"Here's nitty-gritty, [barcode] Christianity in the real world. In [barcode] tep, how to do the hard stuff: fo en yourself to the healing power of God's mercy. If these graces have seemed remote, theoretical, or elusive to you, seek here and find everything you need: a prescription for spiritual health and lifelong conversion."
— Scott Hahn

"For those who are relentlessly searching, bogged down by life, or experiencing the tiresome chase of perfection, *Overwhelming Pursuit* is a must-read! Mark Joseph gives practical answers and thoughtful testimony to the fundamental questions we all ask (or should ask) in life and leaves the reader not only a glimmer of hope and joy, but the source of it. This book is for those who want to reclaim peace again in their lives amidst the chaos, busyness, and unfulfilling promises of the world." — Jackie Francois Angel, speaker, songwriter, and author of *Forever: A Catholic Devotional for Your Marriage*

"We need more down-to-earth and practical books like this, and Mark Joseph delivers. He shares his insights, born of experience, that have helped him live a fulfilling life. And he invites readers to tackle tough questions so they can live that life, too!" — Chris Stefanick, Real Life Catholic

"Mark Joseph has done us all a huge service by writing this book. With straightforward points and practical tips, he shines a light on the reasons we struggle to be both happy and holy, and offers inspiring encouragement and honest insights into how we can achieve what we all ultimately want. I loved this book, will read it again and again, and will certainly be giving it to family and friends." — Katie Prejean McGrady, international Catholic speaker and author of *Room 24: Adventures of a New Evangelist* and *Follow: Your Lifelong Adventure with Jesus*

"In *Overwhelming Pursuit*, Mark Joseph shares with us the very basics of our faith. Through personal stories Mark reminds us of the essentials of the spiritual life: love, forgiveness, suffering, fellowship, and God's abiding presence. Whether you are just beginning on the journey of faith or would like a simple reminder, you will find this book very helpful." — Fr. Dave Pivonka, TOR, author and speaker

"In *Overwhelming Pursuit*, Mark Joseph provides a deeply personal account of his journey from emptiness to wholeness. The lessons he shares will be helpful to anyone who is struggling with the pressures of performance and success." — Steve Gladen, Pastor of Small Groups, Saddleback Church, and author of *Small Groups with Purpose, Leading Small Groups with Purpose*, and *Planning Small Groups with Purpose*

"Mark Joseph takes the reader by the hand to walk him or her out of the stress, despair, and chaos that so many live with into peace and a relationship with God. If you've only just begun to look for God, or have been walking with him for years, this book will help you make progress down the road to the kind of life your heart longs for. Clear, intensely practical, and often deeply moving, I recommend it to anyone." — John Bergsma, author and professor of theology at Franciscan University of Steubenville

"Mark Joseph's new book, *Overwhelming Pursuit*, is both inspiring and practical — a great read for men and women of all ages who are looking for the tools necessary to live a more fulfilled and purposeful life!" — Emily Wilson Hussem, international Catholic speaker, musician, and author of *Go Bravely: Becoming the Woman You Were Created to Be*

"Countless books promise 'change,' but in *Overwhelming Pursuit* Mark Joseph offers practical insights and wisdom to actually make it happen. He introduces the reader to the God many thought they knew. If you really want to have a joy- and peace-filled life, you have to know the giver of life. So, if you're really ready to start living, this book's for you." — Mark Hart, executive vice president content and identity, LifeTeen

"Long ago, St. Augustine confessed the question, 'Is not human life on earth a time of testing without respite?' Even when all seems to be going well, we can find ourselves overwhelmed with the demands of life, and especially so in this fast-paced, technological age. Mark Joseph, heeding Our Lord's call to go to him with our heavy labors, offers us the opportunity to learn from his lived experience. *Overwhelming Pursuit* is a wonderful work which will surely offer many the guidance they need to juggle the demands of an overwhelmed life." — Curtis Martin, founder and CEO, FOCUS

MARK JOSEPH

OVERWHELMING
PURSUIT

STOP CHASING
YOUR LIFE AND
LIVE

Our
Sunday
Visitor

www.osv.com
Our Sunday Visitor Publishing Division
Our Sunday Visitor, Inc.
Huntington, Indiana 46750

Our Sunday Visitor Publishing Division
Our Sunday Visitor, Inc.
200 Noll Plaza
Huntington, IN 46750
1-800-348-2440

ISBN: 978-1-68192-204-1 (Inventory No. T1920)
eISBN: 978-1-68192-203-4
LCCN: 2018943163

Cover and interior design: Lindsey Riesen
Cover art: Shutterstock

PRINTED IN THE UNITED STATES OF AMERICA

ABOUT THE AUTHOR

MARK JOSEPH is executive director of the Christian Outreach Office at the Franciscan University of Steubenville. He and his amazing team get to share the love of Christ with tens of thousands of people every year. He blogs, speaks, and helps men and women who feel overwhelmed by life's struggles to understand that they are made for greatness. Mark is married and has three adult children, two sons-in-law, and a granddaughter. He and his wife live outside of Pittsburgh. His passions are faith, family, and fitness.

DEDICATION

I dedicate this book to …

My wife, Cyndi, whose love and companionship
I could not imagine living without;

our three kids, Danielle, Tricia, and Robert —
I am so proud of who they've become;

and my parents, for being there no matter the
circumstance, always an example of God's love.

TABLE OF CONTENTS

AUTHOR'S NOTE

All of us want to live good lives. We want to experience success, to be happy, and to feel loved. The problem is, most of us don't know how to achieve these goals. So we pursue prominence, possessions, pleasure, and fulfillment in our personal relationships, thinking these things will satisfy us. Probably not unlike you, I fully bought into these false answers for years, working very hard to succeed and, objectively speaking, accomplishing much over a period of time. Then tragedy struck, and I lost my family as I knew it, as well as the business I had spent so many years building.

In hindsight, I was just as overwhelmed when things seemed to be going well as when things turned really bad. It just felt different. During the good times, it was all about the pace: running, running, running. There was always too much to do and never enough hours in the day. It was overwhelming, but because I felt as if I was in control I hardly noticed it. In the bad times, I was exhausted, deflated, frustrated, and very aware of just how overwhelmed I truly was. It was then, when my life reached the point of crisis, that I began to learn the lessons that have benefited me beyond belief. I was forced to my knees, and I experienced true conversion.

As I have learned how to remove the shackles that the world puts on us, I have been blessed with profound freedom, peace, joy, and fulfillment. I am so excited by what I've found for myself that I'm committed to sharing it with others. My situation is anything but unique, and over my years of ministry

I've found that this message deeply resonates with people from many different walks of life. So I've written this book in the hope of helping as many people as possible to find the same freedom I have found — freedom from the false promises of happiness that keep so many of us overwhelmed, freedom to live deeply rewarding lives of peace, joy, and fulfillment.

It is my hope that this book will serve as a resource to you, that it will help you find relief from whatever life circumstances are overwhelming you. I pray that it will allow you to see yourself as you are: a person worthy of love precisely because you exist, and not for what you achieve. I hope that the principles I lay out here will do for you what they did for me, setting you on the path to finding your life's purpose. Because whether you're aware of it or not, you were made for greatness.

Before we can address any issue we first need to understand it, so the first half of this book will look at why we are the way we are and how we got here. The second half is a guide to resolving our issues, positioning us to live lives of peace, joy, and fulfillment. This book is meant to be more than a casual read. I encourage you to highlight what really resonates with you, make notes in the margins, and make it your own. Please consider praying through and reflecting on parts that really impact you. Included at the end of each chapter are reflections and suggested actions, in addition to a blank page for you to record your thoughts and potential plans. Please use these to help you on your journey.

It is my deepest wish and prayer that this book will help you find true peace, a peace that can come only from living a life of surrender, gratitude, humility, and love. As I write this book, I thank God for the journey. I thank him for the joy-filled times and the tragedies, the lessons learned, and most of all for bringing me close to him. And I thank him for you as you read this book, and for the incredible journey he's got in store for you.

INTRODUCTION

Overwhelmed? How about this as a visual? We've all seen the hamster on the wheel in the glass cage. It's probably not hard for you to imagine that, instead of the hamster, it's you on that wheel. You're running as fast as you can and you're out of breath. You can't find a way to jump off. Exhausted, you're dimly aware of the world going by around you. You can't keep up. You're massively stressed. You wonder what your life's purpose is, what life is really supposed to be about. You wonder if the people in your life really care about you, and if they'll stick around if you finally drop, exhausted. You wonder if anyone else feels this way. There's no end in sight. There's nothing that you've found to correct for the chaos. You aren't happy and certainly aren't fulfilled in your life, but there's no time to change course or redirect. Yes, you're overwhelmed.

The scary thing is, if you're like most of us, this is what life feels like almost every single day. You're running, running, running after something, maybe after many things. But no matter how hard you push, you never seem to get anywhere.

With the internet, social media, and smart devices, not only do things move much faster, but we're always connected. There's no downtime, no break from our personal or professional relationships and responsibilities. We have more things to do and less time to do them. If you're a married parent, it's likely both you and your spouse are working, but even if one of you stays at home life is probably no less hectic. A typical day starts early in the morning, getting ourselves ready for work and the kids ready for school. No matter what we prepare the night before, the morning never goes as smoothly as planned, and we find ourselves making the mad dash to the car or the school bus.

The frenetic pace of life continues at work. While we're stressed with the day's tasks, in the background are concerns over our careers, compensation, the needs of our families, funding of college, planning for retirement, paying for houses, cars, vacations, the kids' activities, hobbies, and whatever else allows us to maintain a standard of living, get ahead, or at least feel as if we're keeping up. Then we take those worries and challenges home, where we're trying to be present to our families. There's lots of pressure, lots of stress, and little time to relax. You know that there are things you could do that could bring you some calm, some peace, but you can't find the time or the energy to do them.

Being overwhelmed afflicts just about everyone in today's fast-paced, competitive world. Whether married or single, with kids or not, empty nester, beginning or advanced in your career, a student or retired, wildly successful or just getting by, we all know what it's like to feel completely overwhelmed.

Yet in spite of our exhausting efforts at happiness, we're not happy. We love our kids and love running them around. Many of us enjoy good marriages. Many of us love our jobs and are enthusiastically engaged in our careers. Yet, even for most of us in these more fortunate circumstances, we're not fulfilled. We still want to know what life is all about, what our purpose is. In an attempt to make sense of everything, we try to do more, get more control over our lives and ourselves, and as a result we feel more overwhelmed than ever.

What's Going On?

Take a step back and look at your life objectively for a moment. Do you ever wonder why you put yourself through all this? I've had to ask myself the same question, and the answer certainly surprised me.

The reason we do this to ourselves isn't as mysterious as it appears. We all want to lead good lives, to be happy, to be successful. We're taught from the first day of preschool to go after success. For some of us that means wealth or fame; for others it means power, a terminal degree, athletic achievement, popularity, social status, or physical beauty. While we may operate by different definitions of "success," we can boil it down to one common concept: making something of ourselves.

If we're honest, we believe worldly success will bring us happiness because we think it says something about us. Success lets me and everybody else know I'm important — that I'm worth loving. Success is how I prove my worth in this world.

Just about all of us operate from this deep-seated, often subconscious, belief. We believe that we have to earn love, that it isn't given unconditionally. Striving to be loved, to be accepted, we pursue success. Adults live this out, and our kids pick up on it — whether it is overemphasis on better schools, great grades, winning at sports, glamorous professions, impressive academic degrees, jobs with the best salaries, advancement in careers, big money, nice houses, fast cars, cool gadgets, you name it.

I've experienced this in my own life. I see it among my family and friends. We're running ourselves to death on the hamster wheel of life, always searching for more, because we think this is the only way to maintain a toehold in the world. Because we're trying to create our own fulfillment, we end up surrounding ourselves with superficial relationships, setting unrealistic goals, working exhausting schedules, and trying to fill the void with all sorts of things we don't need or — if we're honest with ourselves — don't even want. The excesses we live with or aspire to are astonishing, often well exceeding our means. In fact, statistically speaking, according to the 2012 National Financial Capability Study, only 41 percent of Americans make more than they spend monthly. Our debt is astronomical, and much of it goes toward nonessentials — expensive cars, houses that are beyond our means, trendy clothes, gadgets, vacations … and the list goes on.

The worst part is, our crazy scramble for happiness isn't working. We're literally killing ourselves in our futile attempts to achieve fulfillment. Suicide rates are higher than ever — a study released in 2016 by the National Center for Health Statistics reported that the rate of suicides rose 24 percent from 1999 to 2014, to thirteen suicides per 100,000 people. The number of people on antidepressants or other psychiatric drugs grew 117 percent between 1999 and 2013, according to data from the Medical Expenditure Panel Survey. Addiction rates continue to climb as well, and the National Institute on Drug Abuse reported that illicit drug use among Americans age twelve and older rose from 8.3 percent in 2002 to 9.4 percent in 2013. Yet we rush on, stuck on the wheel, stuck in this ever-mounting cycle of being overwhelmed.

It Doesn't Have to Be This Way

Thankfully, we don't have to stay stuck. The choice is up to each one of us. Like anything that's worth achieving in life, it will take some real, possibly radical, changes in the way you live your daily life. It won't happen by accident, and it will require dedication and persistence. It will take time, practice, and commitment, but I promise you, it will be worth it. This book is meant to offer insights, practical guidance, and personal stories and examples to accompany you as you step off the hamster wheel and start moving — no matter how slowly — toward true fulfillment in your life.

I'm not a pastor, so I won't be preaching at you in the pages that follow. I'm not a therapist, so I won't pretend to offer clinical advice. What I can do is share what I've learned through my own experience and seen in my ministry work over the years. I've been incredibly overwhelmed in my own scramble for success and fulfillment. I know what it's like to feel trapped beneath the burdens, to try to fill the infinite hole in the center of my chest with all sorts of meaningless junk. I've suffered extreme loss and come to the brink of despair.

Along the way, I have learned how to let go and start living a truly fulfilling life.

Getting from overwhelmed to fulfilled doesn't happen overnight. It isn't like flipping a switch. And it's certainly not the easiest thing in the world to accomplish, but the rewards have been life-changing for me. One size does not fit all, and no two journeys will be the same. That said, this book will provide methodologies and processes that can work for just about anyone.

Moving past overwhelmed doesn't mean all of your problems will disappear. But as you read this book and begin to implement these changes in your life, you will be able to handle problems in a way that you've never thought possible. You'll also begin to experience a freedom that you've only dreamed of, a conviction about your life's purpose, and the overwhelming (no pun intended) sense that you are made for greatness.

It's never too late to start being the person you want to be, the person you were designed to be. I look forward to accompanying you on this journey.

REFLECT
- What does success in life mean to you?
- What aspects of your life are causing you to feel most overwhelmed right now? What things create the most stress in your life?
- Is there any overlap between your vision of success and the stress in your life?

SUGGESTED ACTIONS
- Think about and write down two or three ideas about how you could reduce the pace and the stress in your life, starting today. If necessary talk them over with a friend.
- Are there simple steps you can work into your morning or

evening routine that could help you slow down — that is, turn off your phone thirty minutes before bed, or spend intentional time with your family each week?

NOTES

Part I

OVERWHELMED

Chapter 1

WHEN LOVE FEELS CONDITIONAL

W hy are we overwhelmed? Are there many different reasons, or could there be a common reason so many of us feel this way? While on the surface things look different for everyone, I believe there is a common driver for most of us, and it's deeply rooted in our understanding of love.

Think back to your childhood. If it was like mine, when you behaved or performed well, you received praise and basked in the excitement of your parents, family members, teachers, coaches, and friends. If you misbehaved or performed badly, it's likely the reactions were much less pleasant. Perhaps you were scolded or corrected. Even worse, perhaps you felt ignored or set aside while others basked in praise.

Most of us knew that on some level our parents loved us no matter what. But that didn't change the fact that we wanted them to respond to us with praise, excitement, and pride, and it hurt when they didn't.

For me, it started when I was young. I struggled academically, reading on a second-grade level in the fifth grade. I was tutored in reading for several years. My brother Dan, who is one year younger, is off-the-charts brilliant. My parents used to joke that Dan talked before he walked. Dan got all the praise and attention for his performance in the classroom, while I got none. To make matters even more painful, he was put in the same English class with me when I was in eighth grade. In hindsight, I now believe that my poor academic performance made me somehow feel less lovable than my brother.

For many of us, the deep-seated belief that love is conditional gets reinforced when we don't perform at our best, or when we fail. The way other people respond to our failure plays a big role in diminishing our sense of self-worth, whether they criticize us or respond with (sometimes deafening) silence. Although there are times when things are better left unsaid, silence as a response to failure or poor performance can really hurt. Young people especially sense disappointment, and it's made even worse when nothing is said.

It's also important to note that not all criticism is bad — in fact, constructive criticism can be incredibly life-giving when done correctly. Constructive criticism attempts to help you improve by taking a positive approach, looking both at those things you do well and those things that need some work and how to improve them, without making you feel bad. Often when we fail, however, we receive destructive criticism, which is never helpful or good. This criticism might focus solely on the failure itself, or it could be derogatory toward the recipient. Sometimes it even turns into a personal attack that has nothing to do with performance at all.

Trying to Prove Ourselves

Regardless of the details of your particular experience, chances are you feel a need to prove yourself on some level. Almost all of us believe that we have to earn love, that it isn't given unconditionally. We learn this from a young age, and we take this belief into the rest of our lives. Striving to be loved, to be accepted, we learn to chase success, which each person defines in different ways. Achieving success, regardless of the endeavor, makes us feel loved, accepted, and respected; we feel important, validated. And because we like those feelings, we keep pursuing more success.

My first experience of the impact of performing well was in football. Growing up in Pittsburgh, my three brothers and

I loved the sport, playing it all the time, pretending that we were our favorite Steelers out on the field. I started playing organized football in sixth grade, and in my first year I was a starter. I didn't see much playing time in seventh or eighth grade, but started in ninth. As a sophomore, I quit playing. (In hindsight, I realize I chose to quit because I was intimidated by the head coach, a huge man with a chipped tooth).

That same year, though, I found the weight room. Dan lifted and worked out with me for hours on end. That's when I started tying my identity to my physical stature. I was maturing physically, gaining weight, gaining muscle, and gaining confidence. I returned to football as a junior and was a defensive starter. Senior year, a coach recognized my abilities and moved me from defensive back to defensive end. All my hard work paid off. I was a full-time defensive player for the rest of the season, played an impactful role on a very good team that won the championship for the second year in a row, and was all-conference. I even had my picture in the paper three times that season.

All of us on the team were treated like superheroes. We basked in the praise from coaches, fellow teammates, parents, family members, friends, the school, the community, even the media. I can't speak for the other guys, but I really felt loved. My teammates and I were champions. Everyone loved us … because we succeeded.

Maybe you've had similar experiences. Or maybe you feel as if you've never succeeded at anything. Either way, the fact is, we perceive that we receive love for how well we perform. The better we perform (we think), the more love we receive. And if we don't receive praise, we don't feel loved. At a fundamental level, we all want to be loved and accepted. That senior year, I really internalized this. In hindsight, I believe this formed me going into my adult life.

Of course, my parents certainly didn't mean to make me feel less lovable than my brother. Few parents set out to give their children anything less than unconditional love. Those who care for us, family and friends, typically want the best for us and are happy about our accomplishments. Yet when we focus too much on achievement — whether our own or that of others — we can unknowingly create or reinforce the belief that love is conditional and has to be earned.

That belief is often reinforced outside the home as we leave the safety of family and try to make friends among our peers, or face the challenges of dating, advanced education, and professional life. Today, with the prevalence of social media, the sense of having to earn love is heightened because there's a drive not only for constant connection but to present ourselves as "perfect."

When Our "Who" Is Our "Do"

This sense of having to earn love became very apparent in my business career, where my identity was completely wrapped up in my role and how well I performed. My "who" was my "do." When I first started in business, I had great mentors in a woman named Rosemary and her husband, Ken. They taught me everything they knew about sales. Rosemary later worked with me in my business and has been a good friend for many years. Back in my early twenties, when I first met her, she would talk to me about the difference between our role and our identity. Our role is what we do for a living. It is what we are measured by. Roles could be husband or wife, father or mother, son or daughter, brother or sister, friend, doctor, lawyer, bricklayer, or electrician. Our identity, on the other hand, is who we are as God's creation, made to be great and to live for God's glory. Rosemary tried to teach me that I needed a strong identity to have healthy self-esteem. I didn't know it at the time, but my self-worth then was based purely on the success I had in my role.

When I was twenty-seven years old, I bought a business in the pollution-control and air-filtration industry, growing it from a company of just two employees to thirty in a span of ten years. I worked tirelessly. Twelve- to thirteen-hour days were the norm, plus time on the weekends.

After the terrorist attacks of 9/11 occurred, there were anthrax attacks on United States Postal Service (USPS) facilities, which killed several people. Drawing from past experience, we approached the USPS with solutions to biohazards within their facilities nationally. Working with large organizations that are a part of the postal infrastructure helped us win an incredibly large and lucrative contract that required us to hire more than one hundred employees and rent an additional 100,000 square feet of space. Increases in the scope resulted in additional revenue as we won additional orders for other projects. I never worked harder in my life. Our headquarters were in Pittsburgh, but I traveled a lot to Washington, D.C., and Baltimore.

When my business — my pride and joy — was up, I was up. When I was successful, I was on top of the world, basking in the praise and admiration of many people, including the local press. I felt loved, yet, because I believed I always had to earn love, I was constantly striving for more success, terrified of losing what I had gained. My life was consumed by this drive. The books I read, the studying I did, the people I networked with, and the endless hours I worked were all in order to succeed. That little boy inside of me, even as an adult man, needed to be validated, needed to be loved, and that need pushed me on relentlessly.

I know that I'm not alone in this drive to succeed, to earn validation. We all want to be loved and to feel that we are loved. We want to be accepted and appreciated, no matter what we do or how we perform. But the fact is, just about all of us believe on some level that we are loved for how we perform — for doing well, achieving, succeeding — whether in school, at work, on the athletic field, as an artist, or even in relationships. And because we base our sense of worth on the way other people respond to us, we do everything in our power to ensure we get only positive responses. The result: We're overwhelmed because we feel constant pressure to earn — and then keep — love by performing well.

How do we change this pattern? It starts with changing the way we think about love and what it means to be loved. And that starts with learning to love ourselves properly.

REFLECTION
- Think back on the times in your life when you felt loved. Were those feelings tied to success or praise?
- What are two or three areas in your life where you see yourself trying to earn love from others (possibly at work, at home, or even in some hobby or activity you're good at)?
- Is the desire for praise or validation a driving force behind any of your actions and decisions now?

SUGGESTED ACTIONS
- Think about and write down some ways you can overcome this notion of "earned love." Commit to putting one of them into practice this week, whether with your family, at school, or in the workplace.

NOTES

_____

_____

_____

_____

_____

_____

_____

_____

_____

_____

_____

_____

_____

_____

_____

_____

_____

_____

_____

_____

_____

_____

Chapter 2

WHY WE DON'T LOVE OURSELVES

W e know that we're supposed to love ourselves, but the painful truth is that many of us don't. Even those of us who say we do often struggle to love ourselves properly.

Do we really know how pervasive lack of self-love is? Believe it or not, most of us deal with it our entire lives — the very young, those in the prime of life, the middle-aged, the old, and even the very old. It affects everyone, whether male or female, of any race or religion or socioeconomic condition. It is everywhere, and if you pay attention, you'll start to see it.

In many respects, it's no wonder this is the case. We regularly experience things that reinforce our lack of self-love. Comments and critiques from others can be particularly painful. Many of us can hear ten compliments and just one critique and will concentrate only on the criticism. In addition, we see flaws in ourselves that we don't see in other people. In other words, we tend to look at ourselves significantly more harshly than others, believing that others can't possibly be experiencing the same things we are.

There are many factors that play a role in this, including hurts from our past. For some, these wounds may have been caused by severe trauma — for example, sexual, physical, or emotional abuse — but for many the roots are far less dramatic, though no less real. Examples include rejection, feeling as if we don't fit in, loneliness, allowing failures to define us, and ridicule. An important thing to note about ridicule: we often do it to one another without realizing it. We live in a sarcastic society. If you pay close attention, you'll be shocked by how much communication is done with sarcasm — and if you're like me, you're guilty, too. While usually meant in good humor, to the recipient it can and often does hurt. Just look at the word's etymology: sarcasm comes from a Greek word that literally means to cut flesh. Sarcasm is a primary indicator of lack of self-love in the sarcastic person.

Another contributing factor to lack of authentic self-love is our mistakes. Especially for those of us who are (or were raised as) Christians, shame over sins, both past and present, can be a big obstacle to loving ourselves. We see our flaws, and deep down we think no one could ever love someone who makes these kinds of mistakes.

Failure is another obstacle that keeps many of us from loving ourselves as we should. When we're so focused on success at all costs, we forget that failure can actually be an opportunity for growth. But if we're not careful it can make us self-critical, which leads, over time, to lack of patience and disgust with ourselves. Any one of these things, alone or in combination, can negatively impact our self-love. And as indicated in the previous chapter, many of us don't love ourselves because we believe that love is conditional — and we make any love of ourselves conditional, too.

Me, Myself, and I

Believe it or not, the first major obstacle standing between most of us and a healthy love for ourselves is our own ego.

You read that right. The bigger someone's ego is, the less that person has true self-love. What is the ego? This is a complicated question, one that has been dealt with by philosophers and psychologists for a long time. For our purposes here, though, to keep things simple, we can think of the ego as our false self. It's the identity we create for ourselves, and it's often quite far from the truth of who we are. Keep in mind that there is a difference between having an inflated ego and having self-confidence: self-confidence is rooted in a healthy, honest understanding of who we are and what we're capable of. There is a humility to self-confidence, because it also recognizes that we're not good at everything — no one is. On the other hand, an inflated ego is boastful and always trying to prove itself because it is not rooted in the truth of who we are; it's rooted in the lie that love has to be earned, and that to be loved we have to be better than everyone else.

An example in my life comes from my time working on the postal project. At a time when I had an incredibly inflated ego, this success really fed it. Represented around the table were multi-billion-dollar organizations that employed hundreds of thousands of people, including Siemens, Lockheed Martin, and the USPS (a $70 billion, 300,000-employee organization at the time). Executives; program and project managers; engineers; safety, purchasing, and process people — sometimes as many as forty around the table — looked to me for answers on technical questions. They deferred to me, and I was on top of the world. My ego was in full swing.

Ego is selfish. It's ordered around me, myself, and I. Selfishness and true self-love are incompatible because selfishness says that *I* am the end goal, the reason for everything. The selfish person believes that everything that happens has to be about him. Self-love, on the other hand, recognizes that I am made for a purpose that will ultimately fulfill me and draw me beyond myself.

It might seem ironic, but ego really gets in the way of self-love. Because it's a false self, our ego never allows us to love ourselves as we really are. Instead, the more we work to protect our ego, the more trapped we become in selfishness, pride, comparison, envy, greed, the overwhelming need for complete control over our lives, and fear.

Pride
Ego is rooted in and sustained by pride, which is a high opinion

of oneself — one's importance, merit, or superiority — and it smothers healthy self-love. How is this possible? Because pride is based on a lie about who we are. Pride always needs to assert that it is the best, and because it isn't based in truth, it needs to be constantly affirmed and validated. Pride is really an expression of how greatly a person needs to feel accepted by others.

Comparison

If we're driven by our ego, we're constantly looking for ways to assert our superiority over others, so we're always comparing ourselves with others. To be clear, comparison is not always a bad thing. It can be constructive, an effort to determine how someone does something or how you might imitate a good quality you see in another. It can help you understand what you'd like to attain or strive for in your life. Comparison is a problem when it becomes constant, when you're measuring yourself against others to validate your own performance. When it goes too far, comparison can stop you from trying new things, or keep you from using or developing your God-given gifts because of the fear that you won't measure up to others.

Envy

Taken to its extreme, comparison leads us to resent others' gifts, and even the people they are. This is where comparison gets really destructive, because it turns into envy. Envy isn't just jealousy; it's sadness, focusing on other people having good things. Envy doesn't just destroy the envious person; it can even lead us to treat others badly as a result of resentment.

Comparison and envy were big problems for me for a long time. I was always comparing myself with others, measuring my perceived worth against theirs. No matter the event or the interaction, I would take measure of the other person, assessing who and what they were (based on my own limited measure), and what they had accomplished in comparison with me. My lack of self-love drove this behavior, because I was always trying to prove, at least in my own eyes, that I was better than the other person. As a result, when I encountered people who were obviously more successful and accomplished than I was, I became very envious.

If you struggle with comparison, you need to think about it honestly. The irony with comparison is that we end up equating our insides to other people's outsides. What does this mean? It means all you ever see of other people is what they allow you to see. You don't see their insides, their true thoughts, feelings, insecurities, and inadequacies. You can't see what goes on in their minds and hearts. You just see what's on the outside. So you end up comparing how you feel on the inside — your true thoughts, feelings, fears, and inadequacies — with what others present on the outside. It's like comparing apples with oranges, which ultimately yields false results.

To change this habit of comparing, it's important to be conscious of its place in your life. Ask yourself honestly: How often do you compare yourself with others? With whom do you compare yourself? Why do you compare yourself?

Greed

Because it's constantly driving us to prove that we're better than others, ego can be a large factor in causing greed. Greed is often a response to feelings of inadequacy. We try to validate our false sense of who we are and why we're lovable by amassing more and more "things" — wealth, possessions, power, prestige, success, etc. We believe that these things will prove to the people around us that we're important. In other words, whether we recognize it or not, we think that our things will bring us love. And because they never do, we try to acquire more and more, never satisfied with what we have.

Control

Ego can also cause a serious drive for control for many people. Most people want to be in control. With control comes power and self-determination. With control, we believe the outcome is more predictable. After all, no one likes surprises. A little bit of control is a good thing, but when we have to be in control all the time, it becomes a serious problem. The need for control can actually stem from a lack of self-love. When we don't love ourselves correctly, it becomes important to control things, to have things go our way all the time.

I speak from experience. I used to be a control freak. I owned my own business, was the head coach of my kids' sports teams, and took a lead role in all the activities I was involved in. I was accustomed to having a lot of balls in the air, always running from one thing to another. In fact, I enjoyed it. I wanted to make sure everything was done "right" (which is code for things being done the way I wanted them to be done). Like me at that time, many people who don't really like themselves grasp at control as a way to avoid failure, loss, embarrassment, or anything else that might wound their ego. While I would be lying if I said that control isn't still occasionally an issue for me, I've learned that I can still have peace when things don't go according to my plans, and that doesn't make me any less worthy of love.

A Universal Struggle

Lack of self-love isn't relegated just to us "normal" folk. Even our heroes, whether they be superstar actors, singers, dancers, athletes, or successful businesspeople, struggle to love themselves. Admirably, more and more of them have started to open up about their struggles in a very public way. Take Jennifer Lopez as an example. In 2014, the enormously popular singer, dancer, and actress released a book, *True Love*, in which she speaks of her struggles with fear, anxiety, and loneliness, among other things.

Then there's Bill Walsh, three-time Super Bowl winning coach and author of *Building a Champion: On Football and the Making of the 49ers*. Walsh, now deceased, coach of the San Francisco 49ers, is credited as the "genius" who changed the NFL forever. He was not only a mastermind, but a great leader. Yet none of his accomplishments and talents stopped him from beating himself up on a regular basis, as identified by Eddie DeBartolo, then owner of the 49ers. In fact, Walsh put his resignation in motion after winning his first Super Bowl because he didn't think he was good enough. Although he came back to win two more, his issues regarding self-love didn't change, as those who knew him best have attested.

Urban Meyer, currently the head football coach at Ohio State University, won two national championships with the University of Florida, then walked away, leaving $20 million on the table because success wasn't enough. An ESPN Magazine article titled "Urban Meyer Will Be Home for Dinner" tells the story of Meyer's need for perfection that nearly killed him. Nothing mattered, not even his family, only winning. The article talks about Meyer as "the guilty father who feels regret and the obsessed coach who ignores it. He doesn't like either one. He doesn't like himself." What's more, "success didn't bring relief. It only magnified his obsession, made the margins thinner, and left him with chest pains." Meyer struggled with crippling anxiety that forced him to take a step back and reexamine his priorities. There's every indication that Meyer has made a lot of progress since then. He's an example not only of how broken we all are, but of the real work it takes to discover our true identity, beyond the drive for perfection.

Taylor Swift has spoken about her issues with anxiety, stating, "It can feel at times, if you let your anxiety get the better of you, like everybody's really waiting for you to mess up — and then you'll be done."

Then there's Michael Jackson, who needs no introduction. He came onto the scene in a very big way when I was an adolescent, so I feel as if I grew up with him. I have always loved his music, being a Motown fan since my teens. Yet despite his wild success, now the struggles that Michael Jackson had with self-love are obvious to the world. You can't possibly have lived the life that he did, with all the plastic surgeries, drugs, and bizarre lifestyle choices, and love yourself. He clearly didn't understand his identity as a beloved son of God. Nor could he find joy in his life. As talented as he was, his is a very sad story, but one that offers many lessons.

My point is, no one is immune. We all struggle to love ourselves, and the more we seek to find validation in the esteem and love of other people, the more likely we are to struggle.

So how do we start loving ourselves in a proper, healthy way? It begins with getting out of our own way. Remember: God loves you unconditionally and made you for greatness. Keep that in mind while we work through the next several chapters and continue to examine why we are the way we are.

REFLECTION

- Are there areas of your life where you can see that your ego drives your decisions and interactions?
- What are the outcomes when your ego takes over — both for you and for others?
- Do you really love yourself more when you keep your ego safe and happy?

SUGGESTED ACTIONS

- Think about and write down some ways you can overcome lack of self-love in your life. Whenever you become aware of a negative thought, or self-talk that tears down without lifting up, make a conscious effort to throw those harsh words out. Replace them with words that are true, such as, "You are worth it" or "Your value does not lie in what anyone else thinks of you."
- Take note of every time you start to compare yourself with others. At the end of the day, go back and look at your list. Challenge yourself to find at least one good quality in every person you compared yourself with, without thinking of whether they're "better" or "worse" than you because of this quality. Just celebrate the other person.

NOTES

Chapter 3

OVERWHELMED BY FEAR

Our desire to be loved and accepted causes us to place our security in how others feel about or react to us. We badly want to feel accepted, yet, because deep down we don't believe we are good enough, we constantly experience fear. We're afraid to try new things, to risk, or to invest in relationships. It easily can become a never-ending cycle, in which our lack of self-love drives us deeper into fear, while fear makes it even harder for us to love ourselves because we can't push past it to live the lives we truly long for.

The result: We're overwhelmed by fear. Fear is constantly in the background, negatively impacting daily life, work, relationships, and even health, both physically and emotionally. I've experienced this in my own life. It is impossible to be at peace when experiencing anxiety, stress, or worry, all of which are rooted in fear.

Even more problematic than its impact on our health, living in fear impedes progress in our lives. It stops us from trying new things or taking healthy risks. Fear is the primary obstacle to our being all that we can be. Self-development requires us to stretch ourselves, to go outside our comfort zones. It requires risk. If we don't work on this self-development, we can't improve the way we're really called to, we can't grow, we can't fully *live* if we are always in a state of fear.

The Things We Fear

It's important to ask yourself: What are you afraid of? If you can name your fears honestly, you can at least begin to overcome them. Here is a list of some of the most common causes of fear. Which seem most applicable to you in your life right now?

Rejection: Everyone wants to belong, to feel loved and accepted. Nobody wants to be rejected. Fear of rejection becomes unhealthy when we value ourselves only through the acknowledgment and acceptance of others. This fear leads us to conform to the way we think others want us to behave, rather than sticking to what we know to be right.

Ridicule: No one wants to be criticized, much less made fun of or laughed at. People want to be respected and acknowledged for what they do and who they are; they want to be loved and to feel loved. Ridicule makes us feel stripped of our dignity. Obsessive fear of ridicule can cause us to turn inward, isolate ourselves, and refuse to try new things.

Confrontation: Few people enjoy confrontation with others, but some are so crippled by the fear of it that they never confront issues. This can lead to a lot of misery, broken relationships, and lost opportunities, because real problems that could be worked through if talked about are never addressed. I have found that the closer someone is to me in my life, the more difficult it is to disagree with them, much less confront them, even in a positive way. I've come to understand this as stemming from the risk of loss. Factually speaking, though, this risk doesn't exist when confrontation is done the right way.

Loneliness: Although there are many who have no problem with "alone time," no one wants to be alone all the time. We're not built to go through life alone. The fear that no one will love us or stand by us is very real for many, and it can be quite isolating. Fear of loneliness can take a real toll on relationships;

it can also keep us from being true to ourselves (our beliefs, values, and desires) because we don't want to lose the people in our lives.

The Unknown: Most people love a certain level of predictability. While many of us like some excitement in our lives, we resist change. Fear of the unknown relates to loss of control, things becoming unpredictable, and change itself. We fear it because we don't know what to expect, and we don't understand how it will impact us. Fearing the unknown keeps us from going out of our comfort zones to become all we're meant to be.

Failure: No one likes to fail because of what we think failure says about us: It says I am the kind of person who messes up. Fear of failure causes us to shut down, to refuse to risk because we don't want to go through the embarrassment of failing or feeling as if we've let other people down.

I would suggest that failure is the thing most of us fear above all else. Why are we afraid to fail? Usually it does not hurt physically. Even the sadness of failure shouldn't be enough in itself to make us fear it. I think we fear failure because we fear what others will think of us if we fail. We fear that if we aren't successful in their eyes, then they won't love us. Diving even more deeply, we fear that if we fail, it proves that we aren't worth loving at all, because we aren't perfect. This fear keeps us from trying new things, from discovering joy in unexpected places, and from becoming our best selves.

Being a Perfectionist Is Risky

I witnessed firsthand, in an extremely painful way, the destructive, even deadly impact this fear of failure — fear of not being perfect — can have in our lives when we don't address it.

My first wife, Mary Beth, was talented, a brilliant scholar, and magnificent on stage. She sang operatically and played four instruments. Having earned an academic scholarship to the University of Dayton, where we met, she was on her way to medical school when we decided to get married. Instead, she worked in the pharmaceutical industry for a couple of years before deciding to be a stay-at-home mom when we had kids. Regardless of the endeavor, doing things well was never good enough. She had to be the best. She was a self-proclaimed perfectionist.

There are dozens of examples I could share of how Mary Beth's perfectionism (which was really fear of failure — rooted in lack of self-love) showed itself in what she did and how she was always trying to please others. Whatever she did, she always knew best, it had to be the best, and it had to be her way because her way was the best. Everything had to be perfect and she would die trying. To make matters worse, she was never willing to ask for help.

In the beginning, I thought that these were great attributes. It was wonderful being married to someone who always wanted to please me and make everything perfect. Only after a lot of personal growth and counseling myself have I come to understand that she was trying to maintain unsustainable standards for the wrong reasons — partly, I'm sure, to please me.

Mary Beth suffered from depression, but because of psychological issues in her family, she refused medication. Eventually she was diagnosed with anxiety. She started spending a lot of time in bed, missing events with the family and outside our home. We thought that she was just sick, but the truth turned out to be far worse. It was only after I found her unconscious one day, right before we were supposed to leave on a family trip, that we discovered she had been an alcoholic for several years. The date was July 25, 2002.

By connecting all the dots, I now know that Mary Beth started drinking in 1999, initially just sipping a little wine at night. Over time, her sipping spiraled out of control. Mary Beth was in and out of numerous treatment programs, always believing she had a better way, a better answer to recovery. Step One of Alcoholic Anonymous' Twelve Steps is "We admitted we were powerless over alcohol — that our lives had become unmanageable." Mary Beth couldn't come to terms with either of these concepts. She could not view herself as powerless or her life as unmanageable. Tragically, after years of painful struggle, with our oldest daughter, Danielle, at her side, Mary Beth died on November 1, 2012, just shy of her fiftieth birthday.

Our situation was extreme, I realize, but it shows just how deadly perfectionism can be. It is rooted in fear of being less than we think we should be, and even if it doesn't kill most of us outright, it keeps us from living fully. It keeps us from loving others. And it keeps us from letting others love us. The great irony here is that our family and friends, those who truly love us, will support us no matter what. They are there to celebrate our victories, yes, but they aren't going away when we mess up. They love us for us, for our "who," not our "do."

Sadly, not all of us grew up in good homes. There are some in this world — far too many — who don't have people in their lives who love and support them unconditionally. I will be talking in a later chapter about the importance of surrounding ourselves with the right types of people, those who love us, those who make us better versions of ourselves. It is critical and goes for all of us, adults, young adults, and even kids.

If You Knew You Couldn't Fail ...

I have a plaque on my desk that asks this question: "What would you attempt if you knew you couldn't fail?" Ponder that question. Close your eyes for a minute and really think about it. What would you attempt if you knew you couldn't fail? What are your hopes and dreams? What are your greatest desires? What would you love to be doing more than anything in this world? Where do your true gifts lie? What is it that you feel would bring you the greatest amount of peace, joy, and fulfillment?

Before moving on too quickly, think about what the world could be like if everyone lived this way, knowing that no matter what they attempted, they couldn't fail. What would they attempt? What would they try to become? How would it impact those around them? It's staggering to consider.

What is it about potential failure that stops us from trying? What is it about knowing that we could fail that makes us not want to take any risks? The answer is fear. Fear. Fear. Fear. We are afraid to try because we fear failure, believing that we risk losing those we love and even our own identity if we fail.

Here's the great irony: Failing and making mistakes can play a really important role in our lives. Without mistakes, learning would be much more difficult. It's the mistakes that we remember that show us the areas where we can improve. If we can allow for them, mistakes can be a positive thing in our lives. The truth here is that fear of failure actually causes a great deal of failure. When you're nervous or anxious, you are much more apt to do something wrong. Without the nervousness, most often you would do just fine.

And guess what? The fear that people won't love you anymore if you fail, or that you'll lose something integral to who you are, is unfounded. *You* are worth more than any success or any failure. The people in your life who matter know that already.

God Does Not Want Us to Live in Fear

The Bible contains more than 365 variations of "Be not afraid."[1] The issue of fear is not a new one — clearly, it was on the minds of all the human writers of Scripture, inspired by the Holy Spirit. God does not want us to live in fear; it's just the opposite. God wants us to live joy-filled lives.

On the opposite side of the spectrum, guess who does want us to live in fear: Satan. Satan wants to keep us in fear, creating paralysis. Fear can be so gripping that we are afraid to move one way or another, afraid to make a decision. We are terrified about what people might think, how we'll be judged. Satan uses fear because he does not want us to love ourselves or to love others. He wants to divide us, make us enemies. He is all about division.

---

1 Bill Gaultiere, Ph.D., "Fear Not ... 365 Days a Year," CBN, October 21, 2011, http://www1 .cbn.com/soultransformation/archive/2011/10/21/fear-not.-365-days-a-year.

I never really thought much about the devil as a part of my life until I began to work in ministry. Just after I accepted a position at Franciscan University of Steubenville (more on that later), I remember being home alone over a weekend in early August. I was on the computer, doing some work to make sure there would be a good transition from the place I was leaving. Suddenly, I started to sweat profusely. I felt nervous and afraid. It wasn't audible, but I sensed this doubting voice asking: "What are you doing with your life? Who are you going to help? Who do you think you are? Think about what you're throwing away." I knew this voice was coming from Satan. I don't know why the particular word came to me, but I started repeating, "Believe, believe, believe." After a while, my heart stopped racing. I felt more at ease. The nervousness and fear were gone.

The above may sound strange to you. Maybe you've never thought of Satan as impacting your life. I hadn't, previous to the experience I just described. Through other experiences as well, I now know he's on the attack. I share it here so you can be on the lookout.

Speaking of your spiritual life, perhaps you've not thought of God as anything more than a distant figure. Do you believe in God? Truly? Is he part of your daily life? Do you believe that God is all-loving and all-forgiving? Do you believe that God knows what's best for you?

God loves us precisely for who we are, not for anything we do. In fact, sometimes he lets us fail just so he can show us who we truly are, without all the distractions of what we do. When we fail, we discover that God's love goes much deeper than anything we could imagine or create for ourselves. When we allow ourselves to believe fully in God's incredible love for us, fear just falls away. It can't have the final say anymore. Don't let fear keep you from living fully. Become the person you were made to be — that's worth any level of risk.

REFLECTION

- What would you do if you knew you couldn't fail?
- Are there old dreams or hopes that you laid to rest a long time ago out of fear? What can you do to bring some of those dreams back to life?

SUGGESTED ACTIONS

- Make a list of the top three factors in your life that cause you the most fear.
- Look at your list. Where do these fears come from? Are they rooted in reality? If not, can you do a little digging? What's the truth in each of these situations? Start to speak that truth in your life, whether by writing something down and sticking it on your bathroom mirror, or by developing a mantra you can repeat to yourself throughout the day.
- Sometimes the only way to overcome a fear is by performing the opposite action. Is there a fear you can face down by doing (even if in a very small way) the very thing you're afraid of?

NOTES

_____

_____

_____

_____

_____

_____

Chapter 4

FALSE HAPPINESS, FALSE GODS

Johnny Lee sings a song called "Looking for Love in All the Wrong Places." I believe most of us do that. We also look for happiness in all the wrong places. We all have a "God-sized hole in the center of our chest," and it can only be filled by God himself. The trouble is, many of us spend a lot of our lives, with great effort, trying to fill it with something else.

Holocaust survivor and psychiatrist Viktor Frankl wrote, "Life is never made unbearable by circumstances, but only by lack of meaning and purpose." Without meaning, without purpose to our lives, that hole exists and persists. That feeling of emptiness that overcomes all of us at times can drive us to extreme measures, because we are trying to fill a hole that is God-sized — that means it's infinite. We can never fill it on our own. Matthew Kelly has an expression I love: "We can never get enough of what we don't really need."

For a very long time, I wanted to make money for all the wrong reasons. I wanted — needed — to accumulate wealth and be successful to prove who I was, to feel the love I so desperately sought. Wealth accumulation, material possessions, success, power, prominence ... these were my areas of concentration. It is clear to me now that because I was serving money as my master I couldn't become the best version of myself.

Granted, money in itself is not a bad thing. Neither are

material possessions or success in a profession. The problem comes in how we view these things and the role they play in our lives. Money can be used for good or bad. Wealth can be a person's obsession or the source of significant good.

It might not be money that you try to fill that God-sized hole with. It could be something else — anything else that becomes your main motivation. What are the things you try to put in that hole?

As I have said, all of us want to live good lives, to experience success, be happy, and feel loved. Most of us pursue these things in four basic ways: prominence, possessions, pleasure, and the people we are in relationship with.

Prominence

If we are being honest, most of us want to stand out. For many of us, that could mean in business or career success. For others, it might be more about social standing or popularity. Still others want notoriety for excelling in a field, including education, or even philanthropy and doing good deeds. Prominence makes us feel respected and admired, held in high esteem, and, most importantly, loved. Social media plays into this as well, since most of us only put our best selves forward.

The drive for prominence can also manifest itself in superficial relationships, where we are really using other people instead of truly befriending them. Maybe we desire to be prominent to them individually, or to impress others by the relationship.

Why do we seek prominence? To fill the hole. And, of course, it never works.

Possessions

Look at the houses we live in, the cars we drive, and the things we wear. It's a universal issue, no matter our sex, race, religion, age, or socioeconomic position. No matter the income level or the neighborhood we live in, we value stuff. One indication of this is the amount of personal debt most people have in the

United States. Many of us live way beyond our means. Cars and trucks can now be financed over longer and longer periods of time. The amount of electronic gadgetry that most of us have is over-the-top. Then there are all our other physical possessions — the list is absolutely endless.

We try to fill the hole with so many things that are meaningless. What is it for you? I'm not suggesting that we should go without a house or a car, but instead understand why we buy what we do. Is it for functionality or status?

The above isn't to say that we don't have a big problem with poverty in this country and around the world. We surely do, and the Christian life that we are going to discuss in the second half of this book speaks to how we are called to respond. What I am saying here is that without true peace, joy, fulfillment, and purpose, the hole will continue to exist in our hearts, no matter the circumstances.

Pleasure

When we don't recognize that we are made for greatness, we rely on distraction and entertainment, anything that provides us with pleasure. Far too many people equate pleasure with joy. The two are not the same. Joy is long lasting, not dependent on specific circumstances. Pleasure, on the other hand, is only experienced in the moment. Once the act creating the pleasure is over, the pleasure is gone. It is fleeting. Just look at sex: you experience euphoria, and then it's over. "Sex sells" is not only a popular phrase, but also speaks to this issue, especially when it comes to the objectification of women. As a society, we are consumed by sex. Wonder why there is such a pornography epidemic (in addition to other forms of addiction)? People are trying to fill that hole with things that give pleasure. You'll never be able to experience enough pleasure to fill the hole.

People

Whether we realize it or not, many of us turn other people into false gods. Those people may be professional athletes, actors, musicians, politicians, dignitaries, the wealthy, or those who hold prominent positions. But they can also be people in our own lives. In my adult life, I didn't look up to the rich and famous as my false gods. The people I looked up to (often with envy as well as admiration) were the local business owners and executives in my hometown of Pittsburgh. For many years, I was an avid reader of the *Pittsburgh Business Times*, which included articles on the successful as well as the up-and-comers. I wanted to be a successful business guy more than anything in the world because of what I thought it said about me, and the people I idolized most were those I could reach out and touch.

What does idolizing the people closest to us look like? In my experience, it can be admiring someone so much that you just want to *be* that person, instead of pursuing your own passions based on your own talents and gifts. Or it can be relying so much on someone else's giftedness that you place all your trust in them (which isn't fair to you or them) and perhaps even viewing them as your savior in some way. This is dangerous because, of course, we have only one Savior: Jesus.

The truth is, idolizing other people in any way only sets us up to be deeply hurt and disappointed. It can never fill the hole in our hearts.

***

It can seem almost deceptively simple. We just want to be accepted, respected, and loved. We have this God-sized hole in the center of our chest, and to fill the hole we chase after all these things that can't bring us happiness. We chase false happiness and false gods. And we continue to be overwhelmed because of the effort it takes and the emptiness it still leaves.

There is hope. But we have to stop looking for fulfillment in prominence, possessions, pleasure, and people. Only one thing can filled that God-sized hole, and that's God himself.

REFLECTION

- What are the things — tangible or intangible — that you use to try to fill the hole in your own chest? Are they truly fulfilling you?

SUGGESTED ACTIONS

- Next time you start to get that empty feeling we've discussed, let yourself sit still. Don't try to fill it up right away, but just sit with it. Ask yourself: Have any of the things I've tried before filled the hole? What can truly fill this void?
- Think about and write down some ways you can overcome false happiness and not look to false gods.

NOTES

_____

_____

_____

_____

_____

_____

_____

_____

_____

_____

_____

_____

_____

_____

_____

_____

_____

_____

_____

_____

_____

_____

_____

_____

_____

Chapter 5

WHEN TRAGEDY STRIKES

Tragedy is inevitable.

Tragedy occurs in numerous forms. It can strike as war or terrorism, a natural disaster, or a horrific mass accident. It can be something more personal, such as a separation or divorce, the death of a loved one, a major health issue, addiction, a rift in the family, a horrible personal failure, an unresolved conflict with a friend, the loss of property, or a financial crisis.

None of us can escape it; human tragedy exists all around us. On a large scale, we see suffering, destruction, loss of life, and distress. Individually, we experience sadness, despair, isolation, and even depression. Not all tragedies are huge, but all have an impact. Whether it's short-lived or lasts a long time, tragedy can really drag us down into self-pity, loneliness, and depression. It can be easy to feel trapped by tragedy, with no apparent end in sight.

Every single one of us can point to a tragedy, either personally or in the lives of those closest to us, even if only on a small scale. Tragedy becomes a defining moment in our lives, whether for good or ill. It can be tempting to turn our tragedies and any wounds they may have caused into excuses, preventing us from moving forward, going after our dreams, and taking risks. Instead of learning from them and letting them make us stronger, we may let the scars of our tragic experiences overwhelm us.

I know I've been telling you not to let fear run your life, and now I'm telling you this. What gives? Well, the reality is that we are all guaranteed to experience tragedy in our lives. In truth, part of what overwhelms us about tragedy is the anticipation or dread of it. It is sometimes just as exhausting to try to avoid it as it is to deal with it. We are scared of the tragedy that could be. Yet it doesn't have to overwhelm us. Just knowing that we're not immune can help us form the right attitudes to face it without letting fear rule us.

Facing the Unthinkable

In my own life, tragedy struck me very deeply, in ways I could not have expected. I described in a previous chapter my first wife's painful struggle with alcoholism and her early death. What I didn't discuss was the painful loss of our marriage and our family as it once was. You may have heard that addiction is a family disease. It truly is. I was as sick as Mary Beth; I just didn't drink. Although it didn't start that way, I wasn't always the husband I should have been. I didn't support Mary Beth in her endeavors, nor was I affirming of her.

While not nearly on the same scale as a broken marriage or the sickness and death of another person, tragedy also struck my business, my pride and joy.

When I first bought my business, it was just me and a part-time secretary. Over the next couple of years, I started to add personnel and expanded our offerings. Within eight years we started a systems company that could offer a full range of services, including design, product supply, fabrication, installation, and service. Prior to winning the postal contract, we had two locations and were up to thirty employees, plus subcontract labor for installation. I regularly clocked 50,000 miles a year on my car. The pace was frenetic and exhausting, but as long as we kept growing and making money, my ego was being fed and things were good.

After being awarded the postal contract, we went from 30 to 130 employees, which included bringing on some senior-level people to help steer the ship. We had to build additional infrastructure quickly while running the core business. Figuring out how to deploy so many systems so quickly and getting set up to do so was no easy task. Given my skill set and the relationships I had built within the postal service and with its systems integrators, I was responsible for revenue while others were primarily responsible for operations. We worked together and helped one another on both strategy and execution.

Although we won additional contracts with the postal service for other projects, we couldn't sustain our growth. Given our decision to concentrate exclusively on government business, we allowed our volume in our traditional industrial market to dwindle. We couldn't figure out how to hold it together. Over a five-year period, our company of well over one hundred employees with millions of dollars in revenue each quarter shrank in size to far fewer than its original thirty employees. If we had been able to figure it out, both I and others would have done incredibly well for a very long time. Instead, we failed. The company and our livelihoods from it were lost.

This failure was absolutely devastating to me, a heavy personal tragedy. My role as business owner was my identity. The business had been my baby. My ego was heavily invested in its success. Suddenly, the business I had worked so hard to build was gone. I was crushed.

Don't Miss the Opportunity to Grow

Tragedy can have an isolating effect on us, which only adds to the pain. Although most of us have many good people in our lives who want to help, it is not always easy to ask for help — and even those with the best intentions can let us down when we need them most. They may offer to help and then never be available. There are also situations where no one really can help, no matter how close to us they might be. The end result is that tragedy can be terribly lonely. Perhaps you've had the experience of believing, "I'm the only one going through anything like this." Stress, tension, and anxiety can all be at play. No one wants to air their dirty laundry, and this exacerbates loneliness.

In my situation, given what had transpired in my marriage, my three kids and I moved into my parents' house, awaiting the completion of our new house, still under construction. Even with active parents and plenty of activity in the house, I never felt more alone in my life. Not willing to share with anyone, I isolated myself. I was afflicted by so many hurts, but I thought I had to manage them all by myself. Believing that I had to meet the expectations of others, I was unwilling to be vulnerable, to let anyone know the true me and my many challenges. It was overwhelming. To be honest, the weight of it all began to crush me.

I had yet to learn that tragedy, if we allow it, can be a wake-up call, an invitation to accept the reality of our limitations, to reject the things that leave us feeling overwhelmed, and to start moving on the path to lasting fulfillment. The fact is that we can't control the future or stop bad things from happening. What we can control is the way we live now, and the way we accept all the things that happen to us each day, the good and the bad. The healthy response is to live joyfully in the moment and to actively engage with others on the journey.

There are sayings that we don't truly understand until tragedy strikes and gives us the chance to learn the truth from experience. For instance, "What doesn't destroy us makes us stronger." Another is, "God only gives us what he knows we can handle." It is in our tragedies, our defeats in life, that we learn our biggest lessons. My greatest tragedies have resulted in my greatest opportunities for growth, and I've learned that they can even be occasions for gratitude.

REFLECTION

- How have the tragedies — great or small — in your life shaped you? How have they made you better?

SUGGESTED ACTIONS

- If it's not too painful, recall a tragedy that has struck you. Even if it was very difficult, is there at least one good thing that has come out of that experience? What is that thing? Would it have been possible without the tragedy? If you can, thank God for the good that came from that tragedy. If you can't see any good yet, thank God for the good that he will bring out of it.
- Is there someone else in your life undergoing a tragedy (big or small) right now? Reach out to them today and offer encouragement and support.

NOTES

_____

_____

_____

_____

_____

_____

_____

_____

Chapter 6

OUR WOUNDS

B eyond the overwhelming pace of life and frantic efforts to prove our worth, many of us are overwhelmed by wounds and resentments, and it can be tough to acknowledge or confront them. To do so can feel like weakness. Although this is a definite issue for men, I believe it is true of women, too. Fear of facing our wounds is rooted in the belief that we have to earn love. We believe that if we are weak or flawed, people won't love and accept us. We are especially afraid that if others see our weaknesses and flaws, they will reject us. As a result, some of our hurts can take real effort to even discover, much less resolve.

Sometimes the things that hurt us are obvious. Tragedies, accidents, painful relationships, or confrontations with other people — these things are all external, and it's easy to recognize them as the source of hurt. Other wounds are much less obvious. These are the scars caused by specific emotions sustained over a period of time, such as anger, sadness, anxiety, doubt, or fear, perhaps related to the hurts we received from others. These internal wounds can also be caused by life's experiences, not necessarily one particular event. Emotional health demands that we become aware of these wounds so we can start the process of healing and moving forward.

Trapped by Resentment
Resentment toward those who have hurt us can deepen and

exacerbate our wounds. Most of us have had the experience of holding a grudge. Many are trapped and overwhelmed by resentment. If left unaddressed, resentment consumes us.

There's a painfully true saying that resenting someone else is like swallowing poison and waiting for the other person to die. In other words, when I harbor resentment, the only person it really hurts is me. Even if the other person knows of it and feels its repercussions, the impact on them pales in comparison to the impact on me. Our resentment is very personal. After all, it resides within each of us. It can be overwhelming, negatively impacting our view not only of the situation, but of the world we live in and the people around us.

For quite a while, I was overwhelmed by my wounds and resentments, almost in disbelief that these seeming "injustices" could have happened to me. My first wife's long struggle with alcoholism, the failure of our marriage, her death, the loss of my business ... I experienced a range of emotions — sadness, despair, doubt, fear — and I remember being angry and bitter on an almost constant basis. It was real. It was penetrating. And it hurt, sometimes almost physically. My resentments over these losses consumed me for a while. I felt isolated, embarrassed to share the details with anyone. It was the most depressing time of my life.

There is no question that people wrong us, hurt us, sometimes deeply, sometimes with malice, sometimes not. But when we let this fact get in the way of living with peace and joy, we only hurt ourselves.

So how do we get out of the habits of resentment and hurt? It will take time and consistent effort, but it is worth every bit of it. It is said that the first step in solving a problem is recognizing that there is one. In coming to terms with being overwhelmed, we begin to recognize the issues that plague us, many of which are the types of wounds referenced above. Self-discovery is an important step in healing, and research or study can also be helpful in finding solutions. But healing might also require reaching out to someone else, such as a friend or mentor. Our fear in facing our wounds can be massively diminished if we don't try to go through it all alone. I chose to delve into my wounds with a therapist, which will be discussed in more detail a little later.

You Can Only Change Yourself

The fact is that the patterns of resentment that weigh us down are often rooted in the false belief that other people have to change in order for us to be happy. And this lie has roots in what we've been saying about lack of self-love: If I believe that my whole worth is based on what other people think of me, then it stands to reason that I will resent people in my life when they fail to love me or make me feel loved.

A first step in healing, then, is moving past the idea that other people have to change. Remember, your value does not depend on the way other people perceive you or the way they treat you. Even when people treat you terribly and hurt you, that does not diminish your worth one bit. You can't change other people — you can only change yourself. And because your worth is rooted in who you are (not in what you do, how much you succeed, or how much other people like you), you have the power to take responsibility for your own life, beginning with choosing to let go of resentment and hurt.

An important (and difficult) second step has to do with identity. Our tragedies, our wounds, our setbacks do not have to define us, although virtually all of us tend to let them do so. We allow our identity to get wrapped up in our hurts, tied to the ego we've talked about, and that makes it particularly difficult to surrender them, to seek true healing for our wounds, and to move on.

So what has to change? Ask yourself: What are you willing to change?

There is at least partial truth to the saying that time heals all wounds. It was true for me. As time went on, the pain diminished and healing began to set it. That said, time alone would not have moved me past my many resentments. It was critical that I take ownership of my role in each of the painful circumstances, recognizing that I bore real responsibility for what had happened to me. And that difficult realization took time. My old wounds of low self-esteem and low self-worth, having been unresolved at this point, added to the pain of these new wounds and fostered a lot of resentment. It wasn't until I started the challenging process of fixing myself and, yes, forgiving myself, that I could humbly acknowledge my role in my circumstances.

REFLECTION
- What are some of the wounds you've experienced that still have a hold on you?
- Where are your wounds and past resentments showing up in your actions and relationships today? Do you believe that this can change? Do you want it to change?

SUGGESTED ACTIONS
- Begin to think about what it means to surrender the hurts. Don't pretend they never happened, but accept them and consciously lay them aside, no longer identifying with your wounds.
- Nobody owes you anything. Let go of past resentments, with no strings attached. Begin to remind yourself of these things on a regular basis.

NOTES

Part II

FULFILLED

Chapter 7

DISCOVERING GOD'S LOVE

We've talked in this book about the things that overwhelm us and how many of those things are rooted in lies about who we are and where our true value lies. We've talked about our need to succeed and how it is born out of our perception that we have to earn love. We've addressed lack of self-love and fear, tragedy and isolation, and the reality of our wounds and resentments. All of this helps us gain a clearer picture of why our lives are the way they are; why peace, joy, and fulfillment evade us; and why we're overwhelmed. But it still doesn't provide the answer as to how to fix it.

The world tells us we need to do more in order to be fulfilled. Success will bring us love; happiness can be measured by pleasure, accumulation of things, superficial relationships, fame, power, control. As we learn by looking at our lives more closely, these are lies. They don't make us happy or fulfill us, but they do contribute to our feeling of being constantly overwhelmed. The world's promises have failed absolutely everyone. They always have and always will.

Given that you're reading this book, I think it's safe to assume you're seeking a better life, desiring to better understand your purpose, and are just plain fed up with being fed up and overwhelmed. You're ready and willing to try anything to bring about positive change in your life.

Yes, the world's promises have all proved empty, but there's another promise that never fails. It may sound simplistic, but it's absolutely true: God is the only answer for our lives. God is the only thing that can fill up the hole in our hearts as the ultimate source of the unconditional love we desire. But God waits for us to turn to him and to ask him into our lives. He won't barge in without being asked.

My Conversion

My conversion was not something I anticipated. Nor did I volunteer for it. It was more like being hit across the back of the head with three two-by-fours. I was at an all-time low. I had lost my marriage and my family as I knew it, something that I had not signed up for. As I mentioned earlier, my business had failed, which was my pride and joy, my identity. And I had lost a lot of money due to some foolish decisions along the way. I was a control freak, yet had lost all control. I couldn't hold it together anymore. My world was falling apart. The walls were caving in.

I don't know if you can relate to this, but the stress and the pressure literally forced me to my knees one night in March 2006. I couldn't take it anymore; I broke. I fell to my knees at the side of my bed, sobbing. I couldn't stop crying — I mean sobbing, snot flying. I was a 43-year-old man, and I was a mess. I remember saying over and over again, "I can't do this alone anymore, I can't do this alone anymore, I can't do this alone anymore … " I finally stopped due to pure exhaustion, still kneeling, but now resting my head on the bed.

I did not hear the audible voice of God, but I felt a real calm come over me and the room. I felt God's presence, a feeling unlike anything I had ever experienced. And somewhere inside I felt him say: "You're not alone. I am here for you." I heard it over and over again, as if he was answering me in direct response: "You're not alone. I am here for you…. You're not alone. I am here for you."

Even writing these words, twelve years after it took place, I tear up. It's difficult to truly express how I felt. That was the moment I not only felt God's real presence in my life for the first time, but also experienced his unconditional love. I realized I couldn't do it alone, and I didn't have to. He was and is there for me. A huge burden was lifted. I had encountered God, a God whom I could rely on, a God who loves me. I literally felt different. I was different, now knowing God's love.

That's my unique story, and everyone will have his or her own story to tell, yours just as impactful for you as mine has been for me. If you haven't had this experience yet, do not give up. If I've learned nothing else, I know this: God wants our conversion more than we do.

The Invitation

God is constantly inviting us into a relationship with him. He uses everything that happens to us, the good and the bad. The trouble is, we're so busy being overwhelmed that we often miss his invitation. Maybe we feel we don't have time for it. Even worse, maybe we've been so burned by our past hurts and tragedies that we don't really believe God could possibly mean it. "What on earth could an all-powerful God want with me?" we might think. In many ways, it seems far too good to be true.

But it is true. God invites us to turn to him, to bring our hurts, fears, past experiences — our everything — to him in truth. This is what we mean when we talk about "conversion." It doesn't necessarily mean that moment of becoming a believer, though for many that is what it looks like. For many of us, it means coming to know God in a personal way for the first time, even if we've been going to church or calling ourselves Christians for our whole lives (as was the case for me).

Conversion is literally a process of turning to God, and away from ourselves. Instead of focusing on myself, my mess, all the things in my life that are overwhelming me, God wants me to turn and look to him. Simply put, conversion takes place when we begin to understand that life is better with God in it than not. It is when God the Father, his Son Jesus Christ, and the Holy Spirit become personally relevant to us. It is when we understand and internalize God's unconditional love for us.

There are many ways God uses to lead us to a place of conversion. Tragedy (as in my case) is a way God uses to speak to our hearts. Some tragedies happen on a small scale, while others might be massive and devastating. The size doesn't matter, however. God uses it all.

Dramatic transitions in life can also drive us to conversion, as they show us our emptiness and need. Still others reach a place of conversion through intentional seeking, yearning for something more in life to fill the emptiness, to achieve what none of our overwhelming attempts at fulfillment have been able to achieve.

Other people in our lives can also help us reach a place of conversion. These could be friends we meet along the way, people who really invest in us, or teachers and guides. Some come to conversion in a powerful way at a religious event or on retreat, after hearing a great talk or reading a book that strikes just the right chord, or through beautiful music or other works of art.

Regardless of how we get there, God is always inviting us to conversion, and to a renewal of our conversion. How we respond is our free choice.

Conversion is an intimate and unique process for each of us, so one size cannot fit all. There is no clear-cut process for how conversion takes place. For each of us, it begins at the moment when we become aware of God's mercy, his forgiveness, and his unconditional love.

Recommended Steps

Because you're reading this book, I assume you long for fulfillment in your life, but you don't know how to get there. Or perhaps you want conversion in your life, but you're just not quite there yet. The good news is, wanting it is the first step, and seeking it, as identified above, will make it happen. While the process will be different for everyone, I have learned there are certain steps all of us can and should take to open our hearts to the action God wants to take in our lives. I recommend the following:

- Pray for your conversion on a regular basis. It is a gift from God, and he wants to give it more than you want to receive it.
- Remind yourself often of the unconditional love God has for you. Even if you don't feel it, tell yourself, "God loves me unconditionally." Let yourself believe it (there is nothing truer).
- Pray for an outpouring of the Holy Spirit to lead you to conversion.
- If you are Catholic, participate in the sacraments, especially confession, and go to Mass. I also suggest praying in front of Jesus in the Blessed Sacrament.
- Engage with a spiritual mentor, such as a priest, religious sister, deacon, pastor, or another wise person in your life who can work and pray with you.
- Find a friend who is on the journey, who is willing to come alongside you to love you, coach you, and share with you.
- Read Scripture and do other spiritual reading, especially on conversion and the love of God for us.
- Seek out and participate in a vibrant Christian community.
- Attend religious events and retreats.
- Listen to inspiring talks.
- Listen to beautiful, uplifting music.

God Loves Us So Much

We all want to live fulfilled lives. The big question is how to get there. What I learned through my initial conversion is that we can't be truly fulfilled without internalizing the unconditional love and unconditional forgiveness of God, our heavenly Father. I finally found the only thing that could fill that hole in the center of my chest: the love of God. God loves me so much that if it were only me on this earth, he would still have given his only-begotten Son. Jesus Christ, both God and man, loves me so much that he endured his passion for my sins and would have done so if it were only me that he had to die for. This is true for all of us. And once you start to pay attention to it, that kind of love is hard to ignore. When you start to understand and internalize it, that kind of love changes your life forever.

When we truly internalize God's unconditional love, it sets us free. You can be you, not worrying what anyone else thinks, because it is God alone whom we truly need, who truly matters. You can stop feeling overwhelmed by the constant need to prove yourself, to make yourself worthy of love. In my case, I finally had a clear sense of identity. My role was no longer my identity. I was no longer worried about impressing others, including family and friends. I could now love myself in a healthy way, not worrying about others' acceptance of me. I could stop running like a crazy person after success, wealth, and all the other things that had never satisfied me.

I want you to understand the same reality. You are God's gift to this world, designed uniquely for a specific purpose. There is no other person like you, and God doesn't make mistakes. You are part of God's grand plan, and anything that may have happened to you up to now was just to prepare you for what he has planned for you going forward. In understanding and internalizing God's unconditional love and unconditional forgiveness, the unimaginable is achievable.

Think about it.

Understanding that God loves you unconditionally frees you from the consuming worry about whether other people love you. Understanding that God forgives you unconditionally sets you free from the mistakes you've made and any others you might make in the future. Freed from those overwhelming burdens, you can start living a life of peace, joy, and fulfillment.

It doesn't end with conversion; it just begins, followed by healing and formation — that is, becoming the best possible you, all of which will be explored in the next several chapters.

REFLECTION

- Do you believe that God loves you unconditionally, and that nothing you can ever do will change that?

SUGGESTED ACTIONS

- Conversion is the start of your journey. Construct a list of those you know who are on the journey, whom you can engage with and learn from.
- Reflect and write on what has brought you to this point, on why you would even read a book like this.
- Given what you've read so far, make an honest assessment of your perception of God's love for you. How does this relate to any feelings of fear or lack of self-love you may have?
- Pray for help in putting God at the center of your life, which is your only hope for peace, joy, and fulfillment.
- Conversion is an invitation and a gift. Do you want to live a completely new life? Ask God for this gift. Ask without fear, because he wants to give it to you more than you want it for yourself.

NOTES

Chapter 8

OUR NEED FOR HEALING

C onversion is not a one-off event. While the initial moment
of conversion may have been very powerful for many of
us, the reality is that conversion takes place over a period of
time and sets us on a journey to becoming who we're meant to
be. The next critical step on the journey is healing.

We all need healing. Regardless of who we are or what our
experiences have been, we carry wounds. There are tragedies
we've endured, hurts we've experienced, and fears we've lived
with, all contributing to the wounds we've allowed to build
over time. If we truly want to live a fulfilling life, we need to
allow ourselves to heal, and that takes some work.

The first step is to let it all go, which is much easier said than
done. The process of healing will be some of the heaviest lifting
you'll do on this journey. It requires a lot of self-reflection and
vulnerability. It means examining your faults and failings, your
character flaws, your weaknesses. It also means asking for help.

It may not be comfortable — okay, let's be honest, it *won't*
be — but I can promise you from my own experience and what
I've seen in the lives of many others: the difference when you
come out on the other side is dramatic. By the grace of God, it
is possible. You just need to begin the process.

Why Forgive?
After beginning to understand and internalize God's uncon-

ditional love, forgiveness is the critical first hurdle in seeking healing.

This step is not easy. Yet refusing to forgive keeps us stuck in old patterns of self-hatred, fear, and resentment — all of those things that keep us feeling overwhelmed by life. Not forgiving leaves us stuck in the past. It causes emotional, physical, and spiritual problems. The truth is, forgiveness is, first of all, for our benefit, not for the benefit of anyone who hurt us. It is only when we forgive that we can be free from the pain and hurt of the past. Forgiving helps us to grow; it is empowering.

Jesus stresses the importance of forgiveness in the Gospels. The Our Father — the only prayer given to us by Jesus — includes a particularly challenging line: Forgive us our trespasses as we forgive those who trespass against us (see Mt 6:12).

Jesus tells us repeatedly how important it is to forgive. He even told his followers that we will be forgiven to the extent that we forgive. He knew how critical forgiveness is for our walk with God. And he didn't just preach it — he lived it. There has never been any act of forgiveness greater than Jesus' dying on the cross for our sins. Our forgiveness can never compare to that shown by Our Lord, but we are still called to forgive. Not to do so separates us from God.

By not forgiving, I know I lost chunks of time out of my life. My hurts were so deep and my despair so great that it even turned into resentment toward others. For me, one of the biggest challenges in forgiving was owning up to my role in the situations that had hurt me. Coming to terms with that responsibility required a hard look in the mirror. To finally begin to forgive others in my life, I had to go through a process, which included first forgiving myself. Neither was easy. Both took time. Thankfully, God was there to help me through it, just as he will be for you.

Forgiveness Begins with You

Forgiveness isn't just about forgiving others. We also need to forgive ourselves, and often — though not always — this will be the first step. Not forgiving yourself for past mistakes, constantly beating yourself up over those mistakes, is exhausting. What's more, not forgiving yourself says, basically, that God can do something wrong. Because God forgives us, who are we not to forgive ourselves?

Forgiving myself took a very long time. Knowing how much I was beating myself up over all my mistakes, and how exhausting it was, a wise mentor finally walked me through the following analogy, which transformed the way I thought about myself and my mistakes.

Imagine a situation in which your child gets into a fight at school and beats someone up. Then imagine your child is very remorseful, apologizes to the other kid, and apologizes profusely to you, the principal, and the teacher. And although your child is very sorry for what he did, imagine that you take off your belt and start beating him with it. You keep beating him and beating him and beating him. He is cowering in the corner, crying, screaming for you to stop, but you continue to beat and beat him.

Horrifying? Yes. My mentor took me through the above experience, describing the scenario while I had my eyes closed. As I was sobbing, he explained to me that this is what I was doing to myself every day I refused to forgive myself. It was exhausting, robbing me of energy I needed to be spending on other things, positive things. He explained that I didn't need to take that beating, that Jesus already took it for me. I think it was then, for the first time, that I came to understand that if I were the only person on earth, Jesus would still have taken that beating and died on the cross for me — only me.

Refusing to forgive ourselves basically says that Jesus' sacrifice was a waste of time. God forgives all, so if I refuse to forgive myself, I place myself above God. Our identity is who we are as God's creation, put on this earth out of his love, restored through his Son's sacrifice, made to be great and to live for his glory.

None of this came quickly. It took time. I went from beating myself up several times an hour to once an hour, then to every eight hours, and then twenty-four hours, every couple of days, once a week, etc. It was a process, and a slow one. With all the progress made, I still occasionally go to that dark place. If it is slow for you, too, that's okay. Just take it one day at a time, be patient with yourself, and continually renew your trust in God's love.

God Brings Good from Bad

Many of us wonder why an all-loving God would allow bad things to happen. What I have learned through my experience is that tragedy gives us the opportunity to get closer to God. Think about it: When things are going well for us, we think we don't need others for help or comfort, including God. It's only when things change for the worse, when we are in crisis, that we realize our need to turn to God for help.

If you're like me, you may ask yourself why God would allow us to suffer through identity crises, emotional wounds, and the pain of feeling unworthy of love. I was talking to a friend recently who said that suffering through a crisis of identity helps us know the love of Christ. Granted, without such a crisis we can know on an intellectual level that God loves us, but to understand and internalize it on an emotional level, in our hearts, we need to go through a lot of self-discovery. That includes discerning our faults and flaws. In my own journey, I needed to first become aware of who I was and who I wasn't. I needed to internalize my true brokenness, unique to me, before I could understand and really accept God's unconditional love.

God gives us the opportunity to make a ministry out of our messes. Like Saints Peter and Paul, and so many of the other saints, we all need to journey to arrive at this place with Our Lord.

Forgiving Others

When we're caught up in seeking validation and love from other people, it can be really tough to forgive. The more we can rest in the conviction that God loves us, the easier it becomes to understand that other people's faults and failings are owned by them and not a reflection of us. The fact is, most often people who hurt us aren't maliciously attacking us, but are dealing from a place of their own inadequacy and their own wounds. The more we understand God's love for us and for those who hurt us, the easier it becomes to let go of resentment.

It is also important to take ownership of your own part in any wounds that have occurred in your relationships. Before moving on, I want to be clear: there's never any justification for emotional, physical, or sexual abuse. These kinds of wounds are particularly painful, and the victim is *never* to blame. But when dealing with other kinds of hurts and resentments, "it takes two to tango," as the saying goes. Although there are devious, evil people in this world, who deliberately set out to hurt others, most often the situation is not completely one-sided. To forgive others, we need to come to terms with our contribution to the situation, regardless of how big or small.

This is what makes us able to forgive. Although at times we will express it verbally, that doesn't mean we have to say "I forgive you" for it to count. In fact, I didn't utter those words in overcoming my biggest resentment, discussed below. And forgiving someone doesn't mean condoning or endorsing their behavior. They can truly be in the wrong, yet you can (and should) still forgive them. Given my experience, there's a freedom to doing it. It brings about peace, even joy.

We are all guilty of having carried around resentments at some point in our lives. The person I most needed to forgive in my life was my first wife, Mary Beth. Given what we lived through, the things that no child should have to witness, the tragedy we endured, for a long time I felt that my children and I were sinned against and certainly didn't deserve what happened. Although I acknowledge that alcoholism is a disease, there were things that transpired that hurt me deeply. For me to forgive, I needed to take ownership of my contribution to the situation. I played a part, not an insignificant one. Time helped heal the wounds, but it was only in forgiving myself first, and understanding and owning my role in what happened, that I was able to forgive Mary Beth. Praise God. It was a huge burden lifted from my shoulders.

Getting Help

It is important to bring someone alongside you to help do the heavy lifting needed to find healing. And you need to make sure it's the right person. Given my circumstances, I chose to see a Christian therapist to help me through the difficult healing process. Your situation may be different. Perhaps it makes more sense for you to work with a spiritual adviser, a mentor, or a close friend.

Initially, my search led to two therapists before I found Dr. Elaine. I knew that neither of the first two was a good fit because both primarily just affirmed my feelings and actions. Neither challenged me. My experience with Elaine, on the other hand, was as if she held a mirror that faced me in one hand and a crucifix in the other. We spent our sessions talking about Jesus and Scripture, and how my beliefs and behaviors had to change so I could live a life that would bring me peace. My many sessions with her were not easy. I left many feeling beat up, sometimes mad, sometimes sad. Change takes humility; it takes courage; and it takes desire. Elaine affirmed me where appropriate, but she also challenged me.

I used to be opposed to therapy, believing that it was for the weak, and definitely not for me. Now I know better. We all need healing and guidance, and, given my experience, I am a huge advocate for having the right type of person in your life on an ongoing basis. That doesn't mean that therapy has to last forever or is for everyone. It does mean that you need someone you can go to when needed. There is nothing like having a Christian, educated, experienced, objective person to help guide you through the challenges of life. Although I don't see Elaine on a regular basis anymore, I tease her that she'd better outlive me.

If you do choose to try therapy, the important factors to

look for are objectivity (not a family member or anyone else with an emotional investment in your life), solid education in the relevant matters, and willingness to respect and reference the truths of the Church and the teachings of Jesus Christ. It's ideal if the person is a committed Christian.

Twelve-Step Program

Because my family suffered through the disease of addiction, I engaged in Al-Anon, the sister organization of Alcoholics Anonymous for family members. The twelve steps are not just for alcoholics. In fact, you can replace the word "alcohol" with just about anything else and the steps will remain incredibly relevant and helpful. For me, my replacement words included "power," "greed," "control," "money," "wealth," and "status." Here are the twelve steps as defined by Alcoholics Anonymous:

1. We admitted we were powerless over alcohol — that our lives had become unmanageable.
2. Came to believe that a Power greater than ourselves could restore us to sanity.
3. Made a decision to turn our will and our lives over to the care of God as we understood him.
4. Made a searching and fearless moral inventory of ourselves.
5. Admitted to God, to ourselves, and to another human being the exact nature of our wrongs.
6. Were entirely ready to have God remove all these defects of character.
7. Humbly asked him to remove our shortcomings.
8. Made a list of persons we had harmed, and became willing to make amends to them all.
9. Made direct amends to such people wherever possible, except when to do so would injure them or others.
10. Continued to take personal inventory and when we were wrong promptly admitted it.

11. Sought through prayer and meditation to improve our conscious contact with God as we understood him, praying only for knowledge of his will for us and the power to carry that out.
12. Having had a spiritual awakening as the result of these steps, we tried to carry this message to alcoholics and to practice these principles in all our affairs.

In reviewing the above, you'll see that the twelve-step program is consistent with the principles in this book. In understanding that we are broken and that God loves us, we experience conversion where we surrender to God's will, as described in steps 1-3 above. Steps 4-9 are covered in much of this chapter, on healing. Steps 10-12 are covered in the balance of the book. I believe that the twelve steps are an excellent tool for all of us. I have used them in my journey, and I encourage you to give them a try.

Confessing Our Sins

For Catholics, the Sacrament of Reconciliation, usually referred to as confession, is an important part of the healing process.

It certainly was for me. I had gone to confession off and on during my life, most often connected to my kids' receiving their sacraments. I remember my first confession after my conversion moment. I did an absolute "dump." It was a tearful experience and a long confession (I felt sorry for whoever was next in line, because it took more than a little while). I remember the relief that came over me when, at the end, the priest said, "God, the Father of mercies, through the death and resurrection of his Son has reconciled the world to himself and sent the Holy Spirit among us for the forgiveness of sins; through the ministry of the Church may God give you pardon and peace, and *I absolve you from your sins in the name of the Father, and of the Son, and of the Holy Spirit.*" Wow! What a weight was lifted from me!

The biggest impact of confession, of course, is having your sins forgiven. We Catholics believe that our sins are "absolved" in the confessional when we're truly sorry for them. This means they are gone forever. Leading up to that, the examination of conscience and the act of confessing to someone who is not judging or condemning you are also impactful.

To undertake an examination of conscience, use the Ten Commandments as a guide and reflect on your life since your last confession, discerning where you have sinned. It's helpful to do a brief examination of conscience every day, thanking God for his grace in your life and the good things that have occurred while also asking his forgiveness for those time when you did not live out a true and generous friendship with him. This also helps prepare you for a longer examination before you go to confession.

Then, approach confession with humility and share your sins with the confessor. The priest who hears your sins does not sit in judgment, but listens with love, possibly asks questions (for clarity), offers wisdom, assigns a penance, and in the name of Jesus absolves you from your sins. You can confess your sins with complete trust, because the seal of the confessional ensures that the priest will never reveal anything you say to him to another soul — for any reason.

If you are not Catholic, I still strongly recommend the practice of examining your conscience regularly. You can even go to confession if you feel the need to talk with someone, just be sure to tell the priest that you are not Catholic. And I still advocate that having someone in your life who can help guide you, such as a spiritual adviser or mentor, is beneficial. It may be a therapist if you are in that particular place, as I was for a long while. The person you choose needs to be someone with whom you can speak confidentially. It needs to be someone you are comfortable enough with to share your sins and trust enough to take their advice. It also should not be a family member or anyone who has a strong emotional investment in your life — objectivity is very important. Having that spiritual mentor is critical, especially as you undertake the difficult work of finding healing on your journey.

REFLECTION
- Who in your life do you most need to forgive right now? Is it someone else … or yourself?
- How has not forgiving them negatively impacted your life?

SUGGESTED ACTIONS
- Write down what you need to forgive yourself for; pray about it and show yourself some mercy. God has.
- Write down the names of people you need to forgive and the things you need to forgive them for; pray about those things and the individuals involved. Make the conscious decision not to carry this hurt and anger around anymore.
- Let go of past resentments with no strings attached.
- Strongly consider going to confession sooner rather than later, and receive God's mercy.
- Learn to seek help, and don't be afraid to offer help to others.

NOTES

Chapter 9

BECOMING THE BEST POSSIBLE YOU

It is often said that the longest twelve inches in the world are from the head to the heart.

Different people come to the Lord in different ways. Some who have great intellectual curiosity, constantly searching for the truth, begin in their head. Others, like me, begin emotionally, letting their heart lead them. My conversion was an incredibly emotional experience that, as mentioned, forced me to my knees. It was anything but intellectual. Regardless of how the journey begins, we all need our heads and our hearts working together as we continue to walk with God.

If your journey of faith started in your heart, don't discredit the need to learn more. Growing in faith and sharing it with others demands intellectual growth. There is so much to learn and to internalize. Our faith is so broad, encompassing spiritual writings that cover a myriad of issues, including God's love for us; Scripture; the lives of the saints; the sacraments; the Mass and the Eucharist; prayer; topics such as apologetics, evangelization, discipleship, servant leadership; and so much more. The mind feeds the heart, as guided by the Holy Spirit.

If your journey began intellectually, recognize that it's also important to fill your heart. Our faith walk should not become merely an intellectual exercise, but rather a journey to grow in holiness — and holiness is all about love. Don't just digest information the way you would any regular text, but reflect on and pray about what you read and learn. Really consider how the information relates specifically to your life. What is its impact on you? How can the words on the page breathe action into your life?

What Is Formation?

Whether you begin with your head or your heart, you need to commit to ongoing formation in your walk with Our Lord. What is formation? In the context of our faith, it is understanding and internalizing the love of God and his Son, Jesus Christ, who made the supreme sacrifice in dying for us on the cross. It is comprehending the lessons taught to us by Jesus during his time here on earth, in Scripture, and by the Church, ultimately forming us to live a life in Christ. The sources of information being numerous, formation is about feeding our head and our heart, to equip and embolden us not only to live our faith but to share it with others.

How does this happen? Just like becoming good at anything — our professions, athletics, music, public speaking, and so forth — it takes work. And the more we put into it, the more we'll get out of it. I believe our formation takes place in four ways, all important to the journey. First, we have to start with what we can do individually. (In chapter 11, we'll look at the three ways we grow with others: one-on-one, in small faith groups, and in community.)

Why Bother?

Although you have consumed the first half of this book, you may still have lingering doubts about a relationship with God or why you should engage in formation. So let's quickly review some things discussed previously. We all want to live fulfilled lives. We've identified that we can't be truly fulfilled without having God as a meaningful part of our lives. We've established that God loves you so much that if it were only you on this earth, he would still have given his only-begotten Son. Jesus Christ, both God and man, loves you so much that he endured his passion for your sins and would have done so if it were only you that he had to die for. Jesus gave us the Holy Spirit, to guide us always. God the Father, Son, and Holy Spirit, three in one, love and support us unconditionally. This is true for every one of us.

In addition, you are God's gift to this world, designed uniquely for a specific purpose. There is no other person like you, and God doesn't make mistakes. You are part of God's grand plan, and anything that may have happened to you up to now was just to prepare you for what he has planned for you going forward. God wants you to be happy and fulfilled, and is present, with his Son and the Holy Spirit, to help you every step of the way. You were made for greatness, but you need God to achieve it.

We have experienced what it means to be overwhelmed by the empty promises of the world; why not give our God, with whom the unimaginable is achievable, a chance to fulfill us?

Before providing details, I want to encourage you not to be overwhelmed. Again, this is a process. As I've heard it said, God is much more interested in our availability than our ability. God doesn't expect us to comprehend everything immediately or to do what's needed perfectly. And the great thing is, even the journey is enjoyable — when you are actively engaged, it isn't difficult to spend time learning and growing.

I am not a theologian or a priest. I have no formal training in theology or catechesis. The expertise I bring is what has worked for me based on what I've learned from others and picked up as a student of discipleship, both in my ministry work and in the work I do in the Christian Outreach Office at Franciscan University of Steubenville. My intent here is to share what I have been doing without imposing it as a rule. I invite you to use it as a guide, adapting it as you see fit. Most importantly, persist. Rome wasn't built in a day. Go at your own pace, but go.

Prayer
Your life of faith is primarily between you and God, so it is

important to start building habits that root you in him and in his love. The best place to start: prayer.

Your most important relationship is with God — Father, Son, and Holy Spirit. More important than your spouse, children, siblings, friends, or anyone else, God needs to be first in your life if you truly want to find peace, if you want to be fulfilled. And if God is going to be first for you, you need to be in a relationship with him. It takes time and vulnerability to have an authentic relationship with God. You can't become best friends with someone by seeing or talking to them once a month, or even once a week. Nor can you become close if you are guarded in your exchanges, if you aren't vulnerable, not willing to be intimate.

Time and intimacy take patience; they take discipline. I'd be lying if I told you I have this all figured out. As much as I love our faith and the journey I'm on, aspects of dedicated prayer time are still a challenge at times. And the biggest challenge of all is just quieting my mind and listening to God. Over the last several years, I have worked on honing my prayer life, doing different things at different times, and I've learned it takes a lot of practice, persistence, and patience.

As you know if you're already on the journey, God speaks to us in others ways aside from personal prayer. He speaks to us through people, places, events, occurrences, songs, things we read or see, and so-called coincidences (there really are none).

The fact is that we make time for what is important to us. Important relationships, our careers, eating healthy meals, sleeping — we make time for these things because they matter to us. Unfortunately, in the midst of everything else we have to do in a day, prayer is often the last thing on our priority list. The truth is, it takes discipline to be a disciple.

I'm going to challenge you here. Do you really want to stop being overwhelmed and start living a fulfilled life? Then you need to decide to make time for prayer, because without prayer, you won't get there.

It's that simple. To grow in faith, to grow in relationship

with God, and to live a fulfilling and peaceful life takes prayer. This is the single most important step on your way to peace, joy, and fulfillment. Here are some ways to grow in prayer:

Try Different Things
When it comes to prayer, one size does not fit all. What works for me may not work for you. I suggest you try different approaches and go at it slowly. To start, commit to something manageable, such as five minutes a day. Pick two or three of your favorite traditional prayers and commit to saying them. Then, with whatever time you have left, just praise God, giving him thanks for all your blessings. Do that for thirty days and then expand it, perhaps to ten minutes a day. As you increase the time, you can add in reading some verses of Scripture and reflecting on them. Do that for thirty days and then expand to fifteen minutes per day. Consider using a journal, recording what comes to you in prayer, your challenges and your joys, your thoughts and your feelings.

One additional prayer practice that I use often is to share with God an issue, challenge, or decision that is in front of me. I describe it to him in detail, including my feelings and thoughts on a potential direction. Then I just try to quiet my mind and listen. You'll be surprised how often God gives you the answer in prayer.

There is no perfect goal, but most spiritual writers suggest getting to the point where you're praying for at least thirty minutes every day. Again, please don't be overwhelmed. And don't beat yourself up. God is interested in your availability, and he will meet you where you are when you open yourself to him. He loves you. He wants to be in relationship with you. Just commit to showing up in prayer and let him lead from there. Once you've truly experienced the love of Christ and walked with him for a time, you'll never go back.

Mass and the Eucharist
As Catholics, we believe the Eucharist is the source and summit

of our faith. We believe that Jesus is truly, fully present in the Eucharist. Going to Mass at least once a week on Sunday is essential in keeping us centered on Christ. Outside of Mass we have the opportunity to spend time with Jesus in the Blessed Sacrament, either in Eucharistic adoration or in a quiet church in front of the tabernacle. I find that my best prayer time happens in front of the Blessed Sacrament, and I encourage you to seek quiet time in prayer before the Eucharist, even if it's only once a week. Check your parish bulletin to see whether your parish offers Eucharistic adoration, or ask your priest. If not, pray in front of Jesus in the tabernacle. You can also check www.masstimes.org for parish locations and times for Mass, adoration, and confession.

Confession

It's important to develop a habit of going to confession regularly. The Church states that we need to go at least once a year. I've made a habit of going once a month. I find it helps me to remember when to go next by sticking to the same day each month, such as the first or third Saturday.

Reading Scripture

Catholics are criticized for not knowing Scripture. For a long time, that was true for me. I used to joke, "I'm Catholic, so I don't know my Bible." If we want to grow in faith, we need to know the Bible, which is the living, inspired word of God. Praying through Scripture is the best way to really get to know our Savior.

I started reading Scripture by reading the *Bible in a Year* (there is a Protestant version and a Catholic version). Although you can start it any day of the year, it makes for a great New Year's resolution. It is broken down into 365 days. On each day, you read verses from the Old Testament, the New Testament, Proverbs, and Psalms. The first year, I just read it. The next year, I opted to do it again. This time I was able to pray through it. Reading the Bible like this helped me understand it in its totality, and having it broken down day by day helped me stay disciplined.

Faith-Based Books

You can tell a lot about a person by the books he reads and the people he associates with. (We'll discuss the latter shortly.) When all I was interested in was making money and building a business, I read books to help me in those endeavors. Those books focused on leadership, organizational management, strategic planning, sales, wealth creation, and more. My collection of books back then had nothing to do with God.

Regular reading of spiritual or faith-based books, in addition to Scripture, is really important for our formation. It helps us grow in faith and become closer to God. Find books that feed you, challenge you, and encourage you in your walk with God. I've listed some of my personal favorites in appendix 2.

The journey to a richly fulfilling life is one of ongoing formation, which means, first of all, making time for God in the midst of our busy lives and inviting him into our struggles, our joys, and everything in between. In the next chapter, we'll explore ways to bring God into our whole lives, not just in prayer and spiritual reading, but in our work, entertainment, and everything else.

REFLECTION

- What does the best possible *you* look like — that is, not tied to success, fame, achievement, status, wealth, possessions, or anything other than you being the person you were created to be?

SUGGESTED ACTIONS

- Recognizing that your relationship with God is the most important relationship in your life, make a plan for prayer?

- Pick one book to read for just ten to fifteen minutes a night. I suggest starting with *Rhythm of Life* by Matthew Kelly.
- Do you attend Mass weekly? If not, commit to going on Sundays (or going to the Saturday evening vigil). If yes, try spending some additional time in front of Jesus in the Eucharist for a few minutes each week.

NOTES

_____

_____

_____

_____

_____

_____

_____

_____

_____

_____

_____

_____

_____

Chapter 10

LET GOD IN

I f we are serious about living the life we were made for, and if we really believe the love of God is the way to achieve peace, joy, and fulfillment, then we also need to be serious about inviting God into every aspect of our lives, every day. I've come to believe that all the answers to life can be found in the Bible and the Catholic Church's teachings. Whatever the subject, whether it's relationships, marriage, money, work, character, pride, or anything else, we can look to our faith to give meaning and direction to everything we face. The list is endless.

The Church is rich with subject matter and resources on how to be not only better Christians but also better people. There are numerous outlets, including the publisher of this book, Our Sunday Visitor, that have an enormous supply of good materials on how to grow in faith and as a person. I encourage you to start being intentional about bringing God into your day, maybe in ways you've never thought about before. Prayer is a great starting point. But God is with us all the time, so now let's focus on ways we can include him in everything from our work and finances, to our relationships and leisure.

Giving Financially
Giving has been an important part of my spiritual journey, and I believe it's an essential step for everyone. Scripture tells

us that we cannot serve two masters. Giving more generously helps us understand that we need to internalize who God is and who we are in the right order.

Christians talk about tithing. Tithing has its foundation in the Old Testament, where the Jewish people were required to return 10 percent of their blessings to God. The word "tithe" is not used in the New Testament, but Jesus calls his followers to an even higher standard of giving. He calls us to give up everything and follow him. Some Christian denominations mandate a tithe; some don't. The Catholic Church does not, although it and all denominations have financial responsibilities and need their members to assist with contributions.

We need to give as we are able, which sometimes means giving more than 10 percent and sometimes less. I've often heard it said that we should give sacrificially, not just out of our abundance. As Christians, we believe that everything we have comes from God. That means *all things*, including our talents, professions, families, health, education, and our very lives, are blessings from God. As such, everything we do or have is really his. So when we tithe, we are really returning to God what already belongs to him. And he always gives back in abundance, because God can never be outdone in generosity.

If you're not sure where to begin, Matthew Kelly makes some great suggestions in his book *The Four Signs of a Dynamic Catholic.* If you currently give less than 10 percent of your income (or nothing at all), add 1 percent to whatever your current number is for a full year. Next year, add another 1 percent. Keep going each year until you reach 10 percent. That way, it's a gradual process, and it sets an annual standard for you to strive to meet. My wife and I have done this for the last four years, and it works well.

Bringing God into Your Family

Although there is much room for improvement, I would argue that we live in a very generous world. Many people volunteer their time and talents to help others. The problem can sometimes be that we do this to the exclusion of our families, those closest to us. If I'm truthful, I've been guilty of this at times in my life. For example, I speak about how critical it is to have Christ as part of our marriage, but I'll let nights go where I don't pray with my wife, Cyndi, before we go to bed. Another example from my past life, prior to my conversion, was all the running around I did, being so busy, without first making sure I was doing the job I needed to at home. Now, I have really become convicted that our ministry needs to start at home.

For those of us who are married, our first responsibility when sharing time and talent is to our spouses and our children. How about praying with your spouse before the two of you turn in? Prayers like these don't have to take much time, and they bring you closer together, closer to God. Personally, I can't tell you how much doing this has helped my relationship with Cyndi. It helps us communicate because we can say things in prayer to God that we wouldn't say otherwise.

For those of us who are parents, we know that modeling behavior for our children is an important part of their development. Praying at home with our families is a positive thing, and you can start simple, with blessings before meals and brief prayers with the kids before they go to bed. Family prayers have been a big positive in my family's life. They allow us to give glory to God and to petition him for individual and collective needs. It is a foundational practice that our kids will hopefully take into their adult lives.

Bringing God into Work

Bringing God into everything, through prayer, has made me better at my job and better at life. How does this work? As you plan your month, your week, or your day, offer it up to God, asking him for direction. For years, I've used a day planner by Franklin Covey, an organization that specializes in performance improvement, teaching the concept of solitude and planning. Add God and prayer to it, and you really have a winning formula. Also, consider the following:

Pray before Meetings
When it comes to work, look for ways to make God part of your day at the office, whether you work in a Christian setting or not. I work at a Catholic university, so most meetings start with prayer. In my department, we begin every meeting, whether a one-on-one or a team meeting, with a brief prayer. I'm not suggesting that these things can be done everywhere, but where they can, I encourage you to consider them. Even if you can't lead a whole team in prayer, you can say a silent prayer to yourself before heading to a meeting, or take some time out each day for prayer or even Mass if you have a parish close by.

Another thing you might be able to do is put together a Bible study or some other faith-sharing group at work. You might be surprised how much it can help relationships in the office — and how many people will be interested. I experienced this myself in the two places I worked before moving on to Franciscan University of Steubenville. People are starving for the Lord. They don't always know it, but they are.

Invest in People
Truly investing in people, helping them to become their very best, is a biblical principle. In John 15:17, Jesus says, "This I command you, to love one another." Jesus repeats this command throughout the Gospels. Helping others — and receiving help from them — is critical in our walk with the Lord. Surrounding yourself with the best, helping those around you to excel, is smart business practice, too.

There are thousands of books on the subjects of self-help, professional development, organizational management, and leadership, and while each may be different, most have several things in common. In today's world, it's all about the team, the carrot instead of the stick, training, team-building, positive reinforcement, servant leadership, and, interestingly, many other practices that are actually rooted in Christian principles.

Helping others goes beyond the skills required for a job. It isn't just about performance improvement, but about helping people to have better lives. How can we help others achieve their dreams? How can we love them? So many people are broken, lonely, or scared. The opportunities to help those around us are endless.

Rest and Entertainment

Here are some ideas in another area of our lives, when we are away from the office or our work:

Balancing Life and Work

Maintaining a healthy balance between life and work is critical to living a life of peace, joy, and fulfillment. For me, it used to be about the pace; I thrived on it. I used to work ridiculous hours, run like crazy with the kids, go to meetings, be involved in nonprofit endeavors, maintain a busy social calendar, and more. The problem is, if you keep yourself busy, always running at such a tremendous pace, there's no peace.

Being busy all the time often has a lot to do with lack of self-love and with fear. We want to fill our calendars because it makes us feel important. Peace takes a back burner to the sense of being wanted, needed, and important enough to be in demand. It's important to take a step back and determine why we're doing what we're doing, with an eye to cutting back what's not important relative to your true purpose. You need downtime, time to spend with your family, time to enjoy your hobbies, and, most of all, time to pray.

Cyndi has been a positive influence on me in this regard, stressing a good work-life balance since we first met. Today, we are really about peace. We don't want to be running. Both of us like to relax, to take it easy. Now, rather than being concerned if not enough is on my calendar, I get frustrated when too much is. Our weekends are for downtime. We'll do some chores on Saturday, but Sunday is for rest and going to Mass.

Christian Music

I love contemporary Christian music, so I need only two

buttons on my car radio, one for K-Love in Pittsburgh and one for K-Love in Weirton, West Virginia, the town right across the river from Steubenville, Ohio, where I work. I listen to it not only in the car, but sometimes as background music while I'm working. It's full of God's Word and message, which I find incredibly positive and uplifting.

Christian music might not be your thing, and that's fine. I would still encourage you to find something you can turn to that lifts your spirits and helps keep you centered on Christ, whatever that thing is for you. Those things that we expose ourselves to make a difference. The better the content, the better the impact.

Videos, Movies, and TV

It can be tough to figure out what to keep and what to let go of when it comes to entertainment. You'll need to use your best judgment, but I encourage you to keep a God-centered attitude when determining which movies or television shows to watch. In my family, we have a significant collection of Christian movies with good, solid messages. Most of the movies we watch these days have a Christian theme to them. Of course, movies don't have to be overtly Christian, but seek out content that is uplifting and positive. It's hard to escape from content you've exposed yourself to, so take the time to discern well.

Humbly Acknowledge Your Progress

Formation and growth is a process, which takes time, persistence, and patience. It will not happen overnight. You will experience ups and downs, highs and lows. Sometimes you will feel greatly motivated; other times you'll be stalled. Some days you will feel blessed by your prayer time; other times it will be very dry. If your progress is not what you'd like it to be from time to time, don't fret, and don't be too critical of yourself. Humbly acknowledge progress and know of God's unconditional love and forgiveness.

Some people in your life will embrace the changes in you. Others will question you. Some may even turn against you. It's not always easy, but you can do it. God loves you, and he's there for you. He will provide you with the tools you need and the grace to keep moving even when things feel heavy and hard. He has a plan for your life, and he can't wait to see you do all that he calls you to.

REFLECTION

- Where would you like to include God in a more intentional way in your day-to-day life?
- Are there ways you could create a faith-sharing community in your workplace or social circle?

SUGGESTED ACTIONS

- Think about the people you encounter in your workplace and write down one or two names of people you can invest in this week. What could that investment look like?
- If you're not already contributing financially to your church, I encourage you to do so. Talk it over with your spouse and determine how you can start small.
- Find your local Christian music station and preset it on your car radio!

NOTES

Chapter 11

WALKING WITH OTHERS

We all need authentic friendship. We are not meant to go through life alone, and we all yearn to be loved, to be accepted. We need people in our lives who embrace us for our "who," not our "do." This is truer than ever when we're intentionally seeking to live a fulfilled life. We need people in our lives who challenge us, who confront our weaknesses and hone our strengths. Yes, a big part of formation is what we do as individuals (covered in chapters 9 and 10). But our journey will not be nearly as successful if we don't have others coming alongside us to offer encouragement and help.

We need friends, but we also need to make sure we are surrounding ourselves with the right people. Bad friends don't help us and can actually slow us down on the journey. We need good friends and networks to strengthen us as we navigate life. True, ultimately we can find peace only by being in union with Christ, but real friendships with others who desire the same thing help us get there. These should be people on the same journey, who can walk with us, supporting us as we seek to grow closer to God. Typically, growth alongside others happens in three settings: one-on-one relationships, small faith groups, and the broader community.

One-on-One Relationships
A good friend of mine who works at Franciscan University

suggests a model for our one-on-one relationships in our spiritual journey — that is, we should always be in three relationships in all phases of our lives: we need to be mentored by someone; we need to be walking alongside someone, sharing our lives with each other; and we need to be mentoring someone.

Some of our relationships will be lifelong, but others will change in the different seasons of our lives. Wherever you are now, find someone to walk alongside you; seek a wise mentor. And when you're ready, start mentoring someone yourself. What a great model!

Finding a Mentor
In chapter 8, we talked about the attributes of a mentor, specifically someone you can trust who is objective (not a family member or anyone else with an emotional investment in your life). A mentor should be someone you can speak to confidentially, with whom you are comfortable enough to share your sins and whose advice you would take so you can advance on your spiritual journey. You additionally want someone who is living the Faith and is willing to reference the truths of the Church and the teachings of Jesus Christ. Last, the person needs to be willing to invest in you and come alongside you as a brother or sister in Christ.

I believe that men should mentor men and women should mentor women. Although many have great relationships with their spouses or others of the opposite sex, it's my experience that journeying with someone of the same sex, who is living through similar issues, results in greater transparency, vulnerability, and relevant experience and wisdom, all of which are vital to our growth.

If you're seeking a mentor, take it to prayer. Ask God who he has in mind for you. If no one you know is a fit, seek someone out and consider asking for recommendations from a priest, someone on the journey, or someone at church. If you're not involved with a church, I suggest finding one and asking there. This process will probably take some time, and that's okay. It's an important part of your growth, and you will find it's well worth the time and effort. I promise.

I now have a relationship with a spiritual mentor, someone I speak to regularly, who helps me to grow in my faith. He sees things in me that I don't see in myself and helps me address my blind spots. I don't know where I'd be without him. Although there are some who have lifelong relationships with their mentors, I don't think there's a problem with switching from time to time. Different people can serve you in the different seasons of your life. You just need to figure out what will work best for you.

Whatever your circumstances, find someone to walk alongside you on your journey, someone to mentor you. And when you are ready, start mentoring someone yourself. That's what I'm doing, and the rewards are tremendous.

Faith-Sharing Groups

I once heard a speaker at a Catholic Men's Fellowship function ask, "Do you know that when you ask that guy at church that you've known for twenty years, 'How are you,' and he says, 'Fine,' that he's lying?" It's so easy to turn ourselves into islands. We don't want to share our challenges. I know that this was particularly true of me. On the one hand, I felt completely alone in my struggles, but, at the same time, I was not willing to share with anyone. Then I found a men's group, where I learned that most people are going through very similar things. Everyone has challenges and difficulties. Most just aren't willing to talk about them.

Yet we are not meant to go through life alone. This is why I stress the importance of fellowship, especially in faith-sharing groups, where you can meet like-minded people and be honest about what your struggles are. While I think there's a place for married couples to form groups together, as indicated above, I believe men need men and women need women. Proverbs 27:17 states, "Iron sharpens iron, / and one man sharpens another."

Being with others helps conquer loneliness and isolation,

whether as a member of Bible-study groups, accountability groups, or other types of faith-based peer groups. It provides support in what you are experiencing, education from others, and growth in courage to live out your Christian faith, sharing the Gospel. People in your small group ought to be distant enough not to have an agenda, but close enough to listen, care, tell you the truth, hold you accountable, and love you like a brother or sister in Christ.

Regardless of the specific format, or how often you meet, I am convinced that peer groups are critical to our development, our health and well-being. These aren't groups of perfect people — none of us is perfect — but include people striving together to become the people God made them to be. Likely everyone will be at different places in their spiritual journey. But all ought to have the same objective and be a positive influence in your life. For faith groups, that means having a desire to grow closer to God and grow in faith, working together to become better Christians.

Finding a Group
Many churches, both Catholic and non-Catholic Christian, have small group ministries. Begin by asking around, starting with your own parish or church. If you've already begun to engage with others on their own faith walks, they can provide guidance. You can check with the adult faith formation or young adult ministry offices within your diocese or try searching online. (If you completely strike out, please reach out to me and I'd be happy to help.)

Over time, you will be able to determine which type of group is best, and, as with choosing a mentor, you will want those you are engaged with to be trustworthy. The best groups are ones where there is fairly equal sharing, with not any one person dominating. Finally, you'll want to make sure that the content and discussion not only speak to your needs but are consistent with the teachings of Jesus, the Church, and Scripture.

Friends

Outside of small faith groups, we need to surround ourselves with those who are going to help us be our very best. We need to eliminate negativity from our lives. It is important to be very careful about who we let into our inner circle, which ought to be reserved for our true friends. Everyone else remains in the outer circle, which is ministry. Let me explain further.

Our inner circle should consist of our true friends, those who help to make us our very best. This is a high bar. The word "friend" is overused in our society, especially on social media. While it may not be the language you're used to hearing, most of the people in our lives are acquaintances. To be a true friend takes a commitment of time and a high degree of vulnerability. You need to invest in your friends, and they need to invest in you, each helping the other to be the best person possible. Friendship isn't acquiescing to everything your friend wants, or supporting your friend in harmful activities and pursuits. Friendship is being able to tell someone the truth, holding him accountable while loving him unconditionally.

Most people in our lives probably belong in the outer circle. Now, I'm not proposing for a minute that we turn our back on anyone who is not in our inner circle. But we should not rely on them in the same way. We can, however, look at them as opportunities for ministry. Everyone wants to be loved. Even more, whether they know it or not, all want to feel the love of Christ. Regardless of whether someone is a true friend to us or not, we are called to show them Christ's love, always.

Prayerfully consider your existing relationships, discerning whether those closest to you truly have your best interests at heart, whether they are helping you be the very best you can be. If the answer is no, then it might be time to find people who do. You want people in your life, in your inner circle, who are helping you be your best self, and who seek the same help and support from you. Not unlike other endeavors in your life, you want to be with people who are where you want to go, or are firmly heading in that direction. A great place to find such people is at a church or through faith-based activities. Again, you can ask around for recommendations, including from a priest, people at church, or others.

I'm not suggesting you do anything abrupt regarding current relationships (unless you are in an abusive situation, which you should get out of immediately). It would be unwise and unkind to upset people unnecessarily. But you don't want to be relying on people for friendship, guidance, and love who are not genuinely helping you be your best. As indicated, love them, but look for authentic friendship from those who will truly love and support you.

Saints and Role Models

The saints are men and women who led heroic and impactful lives, heroes of the Faith who the Church tells us are now in heaven. Many other people throughout history, who are not called "saint," also lived virtuous, Christ-centered lives, providing great examples for us. Learning about their lives can be a great help to us as we continue on our journey.

Those who work in professional development and related fields recommend finding someone you aspire to be like and emulating that person. Unfortunately, too often we emulate people who aren't good examples. I suggest that we aspire to be like the saints and heroes of the Faith. Even better, since we believe that those who are in heaven are fully alive — even more alive than we are — we can get to know the saints personally and ask them to help us as we make this journey. The best thing is that, as we become better friends with the saints, they help us become better friends with Jesus Christ, who is ultimately the best friend any of us can ever have. I encourage you to read about them and, yes, emulate them.

Favorite Saints
As I've grown in my faith, I've come to really appreciate the saints, not only as role models, but also as intercessors. At the top of my list are Mary, mother of Our Lord, and Joseph,

her husband and Jesus' foster father, who both exemplify obedience, humility, docility, and love. Both are shining examples for us, and we have no better friend in heaven, other than Jesus himself, than Mary, our Blessed Mother.

Two others whose stories I love are Saints Peter and Paul, both of whom were serious sinners; Peter denied Christ, and Paul killed Christians. Yet both experienced conversion, said yes, and became great, courageous leaders in the early Church. Thinking about these two men and how they were chosen, despite sinning so gravely, reminds me of my own journey and how Jesus picked me, despite my faults and flaws. Saints Peter and Paul show us that no matter how badly we've sinned, not only is there redemption, God still wants to bring us to greatness.

I'm also a fan of Saint Mark the Evangelist, my patron saint. There are no coincidences in life, and I believe that I was named Mark for a reason, called to share the Good News through this book, my ministry, and the work I do at Franciscan University. Like Saint Mark, I'm called to evangelize and to help people on their journeys of discipleship.

Every morning, I pray to each of these saints by name, along with some others. They are great intercessors. I encourage you to pick your favorite saints and do the same.

Community

There is nothing that affirms who you are or what you're doing more than a large crowd of people participating in the same events or activities as you. Examples include professional sports, concerts, political conventions, and conferences of various kinds. Participating individuals feel a sense of belonging and of acceptance from those around them. The same is true for those on a faith journey.

Although I am Catholic, I've intentionally tried to write this book for all Christians — and, really, all people. Regardless of denomination, I believe that regular, communal worship is critical to our faith journeys. Community is important, and so is worshiping God with others. It affirms us in our faith. It also gives God the glory he deserves.

As Catholics, we attend Mass at least weekly. In addition to worshiping together, many churches provide opportunities for faith formation and service. Other opportunities to worship or learn communally include Eucharistic adoration (for Catholics), nights of worship, Christian concerts, conferences or gatherings, and talks. I encourage you to seek out opportunities to be part of a church community in a meaningful way. We are not meant to go through this world alone. We need to surround ourselves with those who are going to help make us better.

Jesus Christ, the Ultimate Friend

Jesus Christ is the greatest leader in human history. There has never been anyone more loving, more courageous, bolder, more exciting, more committed, or more compassionate. Different denominations of Christians differ on certain things, yes, but the thing that we can certainly agree on is that Jesus is our Lord, our Savior, our King. No one deserves more gratitude or adoration. There's no better role model for any of us. Even more importantly, there's no better friend. If Jesus is walking alongside you in your journey (and if you ask him, you can count on it: he's there, even when you don't feel it), you can have complete confidence that you're on the right path.

REFLECTION

- Who are your closest friends and why? Do they help you be the best version of yourself?
- Is there someone in your life who can walk alongside you as a mentor on your faith journey? If not, where can you go to find such a person?

SUGGESTED ACTIONS

- Look into a small faith group at your parish, in addition to opportunities to worship and learn as a community. Commit to joining one, if your schedule permits.
- Seek out a good mentor, perhaps someone from your parish, a small faith group, or elsewhere. If you don't know whom to ask, seek advice from your pastor or close friends who understand your situation.

NOTES

Chapter 12

PURSUING THE PATH TO PEACE

Conversion, once begun, is an ongoing process, a journey into deeper freedom. The moment of conversion is just the beginning. Now we have to let it shape the rest of our lives, knowing that God is there with us every step of the way.

Over the years, I have identified four key attributes that are necessary for continued development as we walk with God. These are critical steps on the path to peace, steps we must commit to every single day. The four steps are surrender, gratitude, humility, and love. These four in combination are the secret to a deeply fulfilling life, helping us move past feeling overwhelmed, no matter what life might bring.

Surrender
The first step in getting beyond being overwhelmed is surrender. Prior to defining it, let's discuss two things related specifically to it.

It's a simple fact: We cannot control life, no matter how much we try. None of us can. I came to this realization the hard way. I was so tightly wound, trying to control Mary Beth and her addiction, trying to control my company and everyone in it, trying to keep track of my kids and their needs, and in the end it all came tumbling down.

Many of you might be thinking it isn't true that we have no control. With a good plan and solid people around you, it's possible to control things. Sure, when it comes to things and planned events we have a certain amount of control, as long as we allow for contingencies, but even then, things don't always go perfectly. Most of life is beyond our control. Other people and their choices and behavior are beyond our control. Tragic events, disease, accidents — these things are all way outside the scope of our control.

Second, and as established previously, we have God, who loves us more than we can imagine; who wants to see us happy; who designed us for a specific purpose, uniquely and individually; who knows what is best for us — the God who made us for greatness.

So, let's look at this objectively: God loves us unconditionally. We cannot control anything (not really). We're overwhelmed by what the world offers us as solutions to our fears of not being loved … so why not surrender to the God of the universe, who is all-powerful, almighty, and all-loving?

Instead of conceiving of something on my own, relying on myself to get it done, and then facing the consequences alone, I can choose to follow God's will, discerning what he wants for my life and particular situations, and rely on him for whatever happens. I then use my unique, God-given gifts to do my very best, leaving everything up to him and understanding that everything in life is part of his grand plan. As long as I know his love, it just doesn't matter what others think.

God our Father loves us absolutely; handing it all over to him brings incredible relief. In my case, surrender removed the pressure. It wasn't just me alone who was responsible. I no longer had to own the outcome. Surrender leads to peace, because it allows us to live in reality. All we can do is give every action our best, using our God-given talents, remaining open to his will, and leaving the outcome to him.

Gratitude

The next key step on the road to lasting peace is gratitude. Be thankful. More than that, believe that everything happens for a reason, that there are no coincidences in life. It's true. Everything is part of God's plan. So live in a place of gratitude; be grateful for everything that happens, even the crises in your life.

Without surrender, it is very difficult, if not impossible, to live in a place of gratitude. We need to remember that God knows us better than we know ourselves and loves us more than we can comprehend. He wants only the best for us. We can trust in that absolutely, regardless of life's obstacles and challenges. Surrender teaches us to let go of the need to have things our way. Gratitude allows us to look past any short-term pain and be grateful for what God wants to do with it for our good.

Everything does happen for a reason, and gratitude gives us the right lens to see this reality throughout our lives. I have described to you the significant tragedy that my family and I experienced in our lives. With my first wife's addiction, we truly lived through a war. What we endured was overwhelming and exhausting. In addition, I lost my business, which I had worked on so hard for so long. Yet I am grateful for *all* of these things, because I know that without these specific experiences I would not be who I am today. If it weren't for the life I've lived and the experiences I've had, I wouldn't be writing this book or launching a ministry geared toward helping others. I know I can thank God for it all.

What does an attitude of gratitude look like? It is first trusting that everything happens for a reason, the good and the bad. It is having a grateful heart and thanking God for our many blessings, big or small.

Gratitude isn't just good for the soul; it's good for the body, too. Experts are constantly talking about the benefits of living a life of gratitude, including being happier, healthier, more optimistic, more spiritual, a better friend, a better boss, and many other good outcomes. To live a fulfilled life, one of peace and joy, you need to have a grateful heart. Without it, peace and joy are impossible. Do not confuse what I'm saying with feeling happy all the time. The truly grateful person knows how to say "thank you" even when feeling miserable. A true attitude of gratitude is one that allows us to see the hand of God in all things and to trust that everything will turn out for the best.

Humility

The next step is humility. To me, humility is the opposite of ego, which we previously defined as our false self, the identity we create that is often far from the truth of who we are. The humble person lives from the truth of who he is and can step back from the chaos of trying to prove himself to others, rather than letting life overwhelm him.

Humility is a widely misunderstood attribute. It does not mean disliking yourself or believing you're a bad person. It does not mean that you don't believe in yourself or have no self-confidence. It may sound counterintuitive, but a humble person has a sense of self-worth, believes in himself, even loves himself, and doesn't live in fear. Humility has much to do with self-love. This is because humility helps us know exactly who we are, with all of our weaknesses, yes, and even more with all of the strengths given to us by God.

Those who have a healthy self-love have no need to look down on anyone, nor do they look up at anyone except Jesus Christ. Stated differently, with the exception of Jesus Christ, who is our Lord and Savior, we are no better or worse than anyone on this earth. We were all created by the same God, with the same perfection, in his image and likeness. To God, we are all tens.

Yes, some people are further along in their spiritual journeys. Yes, we can aspire to be like those who exemplify skills or traits that we would like to grow in, that are important for building strong character. But we are not to look at others as gods. We only have one God. Healthy self-love lets us admire others for their accomplishments without being envious or jealous, and without idolizing them. The person with healthy self-love understands his worth as a child of God, created for a specific purpose. Healthy self-love means understanding this, surrendering to God's will, and using God's gifts for his glory.

A humble person is genuinely happy for others in their successes. He is accepting of others' ideas and thoughts (accepting doesn't mean always agreeing) and is willing to engage in dialogue and even friendly debate. The humble person does not always have to be right, does not always have to be in control, does not always have to win. Humility allows us to accept others for who they are, rather than judging them or trying to change them.

Humility means accepting and loving others without conditions. This does not mean we shouldn't discern right from wrong, but we must never condemn others. Being humble is understanding that it is only in God working through us that we can perform or achieve anything worthwhile. It is his doing, not ours.

On my journey, I couldn't get to humble until I was broken. To humble me, God had to let me crash, which meant that I first needed to experience a climb to the top (or at least what felt like the top to me). When it all came tumbling down, I couldn't hide from the reality of who I was anymore. While it hurt a lot at the time, I can tell you now, it's amazing how much humility sets a person free.

Love

The final step (and the ultimate goal of this journey) is love. Above all else, we are called to love. Jesus tells us to love our neighbors as ourselves, second only to loving God with our whole heart, mind, soul, and strength. We need to love. When we fail to love, we leave those around us empty, and we are empty, too. Yet we certainly can't love others if we can't accept them, if we're always competing with them or judging them. We can't love them if we always have to be right or always have to be on top.

Without relationships, life is meaningless. True relationship is impossible without love. To love, we need to be vulnerable, we need to trust, we need to care. Having gratitude for the people in our lives is vital to loving them. And gratitude brings joy, which is also essential to love.

As I have learned since my conversion, you cannot truly love others unless you first love yourself. It can be a slow journey, but practicing surrender, gratitude, and humility strengthens and confirms us in who we are, which opens us up to loving ourselves and others.

Say No to Fear

To take these four steps to true peace and fulfillment, we have to let go of fear. We discussed fear in detail in chapter 3: God does not want us to live in fear. God wants us to live in the moment, neither looking back to yesterday nor worrying about tomorrow. Fear stops us from being all that we can be. It paralyzes us. It stifles us. There will always be moments of fear, but the farther we walk in our journey with God, the more important it will be to recognize and reject fear when it comes up in our lives.

How do we do this? By keeping hearts and minds fixed on God's unconditional love and forgiveness. When we start to drift into fear, we have to stop looking at ourselves for safety and answers. Instead, the only helpful response is to look up. Understanding and internalizing God's unconditional love is critical to removing the shackles of fear, and we have to remind ourselves of this great love every day.

I still experience fear from time to time. To combat it, as part of my prayer every morning I pray, "Lord Jesus, help me to feel your unconditional love and unconditional forgiveness, fully internalizing and living these gifts, so that with Holy Spirit boldness, using my God-given talents, not caring what anyone on this earth thinks of me, I can be all that you want me to be, in serving you."

It's a Journey

We've all heard that life is a journey. Well, with God, life is a grand and glorious journey, one each of us needs to go through, recognizing that it is lifelong. The journey is not a race; it is born of our experiences, the good and the bad. Maybe you're not where you want to be yet. That's okay — a spiritual journey isn't about "making it." Conversion is an ongoing thing. Allow yourself to humbly recognize how far you've come, how far God's grace has brought you, instead of beating yourself up for what you have not yet achieved.

As we all know, life isn't easy. Misfortunes and tragedies happen, whether we have faith or not. Those without faith have to suffer through the pain with no rhyme or reason. Knowing the unconditional, saving love of God gives reason and meaning even to our toughest trials. No matter what might happen, we can live fulfilled lives. With faith, there is nothing, and absolutely no one, that can steal our joy.

That's peace.

That's heaven on earth.

REFLECTION

• Are you able to accept that conversion is an ongoing journey, one that will require your daily recommitment? If not, what fear or other obstacle might be holding you back?

SUGGESTED ACTIONS

• Make two lists. On the first, write the ways you have not done or been the following, followed by a list of ways you can do or be the following:
    a. Surrender to God in all you do
    b. Have an attitude of gratitude
    c. Be humble in your endeavors
    d. Live a life of love
• Is one of the four above harder for you than the rest? Why?
• As part of your daily prayers, consider adding one or both of the two prayers in the appendix, both of which ask God's help in living each day with surrender, gratitude, humility, and love.

NOTES

Chapter 13

CALLED TO GREATNESS

You may be wondering: Now what? You've taken some
radical steps out of old patterns of thinking and behaving;
you're on a good path and, hopefully, feeling less overwhelmed.
These are good things. But perhaps you're still feeling as if
there should be more. Is this it?

No!

Now comes the really amazing part. God made you for
greatness. He has gifted you with a special purpose. He made
you with special gifts and talents, and he knows you as no one
else does. In Jeremiah 1:5, the Lord tells us, "Before I formed
you in the womb, I knew you, / and before you were born I
consecrated you; / I appointed you a prophet to the nations."
God made you in a certain way for a reason. He made you for
greatness.

Greatness here is not defined as wealth or power or
prominence; it's not notoriety or fame; it's not athletic,
academic, artistic, physical, social, or any other kind of
achievement. The greatness we are talking about is being the
very best you can be with the significant gifts God has given
you. It means responding with a full YES to whatever God
is asking of you today, in your present circumstances. You'll
know you're on the right track because when you start living
this way, you'll no longer feel overwhelmed. Instead, you'll
be fulfilled, pursuing the things that God calls you to, those

things consistent with your gifts and passions.

God loves you more than you will ever know, no matter what you've ever done. He loves you more than you love yourself, more than anyone on this earth can love you. He loves you perfectly, and he wants the very best for you. He wants nothing less for you than happiness, to be fulfilled beyond belief. God wants you to have immense joy and to live a life of deep and lasting peace.

I believe the above not only because it's what the Church teaches and Scripture says, but because I have profoundly experienced it in my own life. God wants us to lead peace-filled lives, to be happy and fulfilled.

I'm not suggesting that coming to this place of faith forever takes away any sense of worry or anxiety. In fact, being at peace in doing God's will doesn't always "feel" the way we think it should. But it does mean we are at peace on a deep spiritual level, that we experience joy regardless of anything that's going on, regardless of the challenges.

Although I don't know how to articulate it perfectly, for me, no longer being overwhelmed by life means there is a calm, a peace, a joy that I never experienced before. I still experience challenges in life, but whereas I used to be excitable and easily angered prior to my conversion, very little really phases me now, which I can only attribute to truly knowing the love of God and surrendering to his will.

Discerning God's Purpose for Your Life

Our identity is not what we do, but who we are as God's creation, put on this earth out of his love and his Son's sacrifice, made to be great and to live for God's glory. God is all-knowing and all-powerful. He doesn't make mistakes. That means he didn't make a mistake in the way he formed you. You are a very special gift from God, made by God in his likeness. You are perfectly who he made you to be.

In his love for us, God designed each of us with a unique purpose and calling. He invites each of us to join him in his work in some way, and it's only when we begin to tap into that unique calling — whatever it may be — that we can live and flourish fully. Even here, what we "do for God" is not who we are. Our "who" is never our "do," even when we're endeavoring to follow God's will. This is a trap that is easy to fall into, bringing our old belief system into our new way of life. I know, because it happens to me. In prayer and in talking to my mentor, I am reminded regularly that I need to "be" with God rather than to "do" for God. The truth is that God made us to share in his creative activity, and when we can enter it fully, secure in our identity as his children, we find real, lasting joy.

So, how do we know what we are to do, what is going to give us joy and peace and allow us to be fulfilled? The answer is twofold: We need to surrender to God and prayerfully discern his call for our lives.

Throughout this book, I've talked a lot about surrender. Until we learn to surrender, we'll be stuck in patterns of living that leave us feeling overwhelmed and empty. There's no other solution to fulfillment. Surrender means letting go of old ideas, fears, self-doubt. It means placing these things in God's hands, trusting him to take care of everything.

How to Discern

Discernment means watching and listening for God's movement and direction in our lives. This is done first of all through prayer. In addition, we need to watch for the ways God is speaking to us through the daily happenings and encounters of our lives, through people, places, things, events, music, books, and just about anything else. In other words, discernment is learning to pay attention. It's also living in gratitude, understanding that there are no coincidences in life, that all happens for a reason. It's having humility in all that we do, understanding that our accomplishments are not ours, but rather what God accomplishes through us. The more we learn to discern, the more we are able to live in a place of love, having internalized our true call from the Lord in all that we do.

Maybe that sounds a little daunting. Do not be afraid! Thankfully, over the years I have learned that, while discernment is highly individual and unique for each of us, there are some practical steps we can take in discerning our life's focus and purpose.

One of my favorite books is *Rhythm of Life* by Matthew Kelly, in which he articulates not only how to find our passions, but how to create a rhythm for our lives, becoming the "best version of ourselves." Kelly talks about discovering our "genius" — that is, the one thing that we can do better than anyone else in the world, the one thing that makes sense "regardless of the outcome or other people's opinions." He points out that many people don't pursue their genius because of opinions of family and friends, or lack of financial reward or notoriety. Yet we can't be happy trying to be someone else, trying to leverage others' gifts for ourselves instead of putting our own God-given gifts to use. Kelly says, "Success is to become who you truly are."

What are your true talents, desires, and needs? Matthew Kelly argues that where these three intersect is where your true genius lies, the "best version of yourself." What are you most passionate about? What is the one thing that, regardless of successes or failures, you could still get up in the morning and do with vigor and enthusiasm? Take these questions to prayer. Detail to God your thoughts on your talents, desires, and needs. Discuss with him your ideas on how they combine to form your genius. Then listen. If you're like me, you won't hear the audible voice of God, but you'll know he's present and feel him speaking to you. Journal through the process and as you begin to discover the things that are most deeply rooted in your heart, you'll find that these are the key to becoming everything God made you to be, and the key to your fulfillment.

Answering the Call

That's how I landed in my current job as executive director of the Christian Outreach Office at Franciscan University of

Steubenville in Ohio. I was praying and thinking a lot at the time about my calling and work. On April 25, 2012, I received an email that caught my attention. It was from Mark Nehrbas, my predecessor at the university. He and I had met through Catholic Men's Fellowship, and he was sending a job posting to me. I immediately called to question him about the job. (One of many "holy coincidences" pointed out to me by Mark was that we two Marks were talking to one another on the feast day of Saint Mark the Apostle.)

The university wanted their new executive director to be a business guy who was a mission fit. The job responsibilities matched my experience almost exactly. After a long series of interviews, I was offered the position, but there was a catch. The new job would provide far less money than I had been making. Having owned my own business for so many years, and later working for organizations where I had an equity stake and no cap on my income, going to work for a Catholic university would change everything. Not only that, but I would no longer own a business (or a piece of a business) for which I could cash in the equity. Making this move would be a huge departure from my past, both financially and operationally. Even so, I felt compelled to take the position.

In prayer, I became convinced that it was the right move, that God was calling me to do it. I sensed God saying to me: "Mark, I know you know that I love you unconditionally and will always forgive you unconditionally, but it's time to put up or shut up. What do you want to do?"

One of the things I began to understand is that there are no coincidences in life, that all happens for a reason. A detail I take as further proof that God's hand was behind my acceptance of the job: The offer letter I received was dated July 25, 2012. If you recall, it was July 25, 2002, when my life was turned upside down with the discovery of my first wife's addiction. It was ten years to the day that I went from the depths of despair to working for the Church, in a job that God seemed to have designed for me.

Rest assured, doing God's will does not mean you have to work for the Church or in ministry on a full-time basis. All of us have the opportunity to show the love of Christ to others wherever we are, whether at work, in our homes, in the community, or elsewhere. In fact, given the path that society has been on for some time now, the need is great for followers of Jesus to work in the secular world and bring Christ to the people they meet there. You don't have to be in ministry to do ministry. We have the opportunity to share the love of Christ everywhere.

What It Means for You

Maybe you're pretty established in your career, so you have a good feel for your unique genius. You may know your desires, needs, and talents very well. That's great! Use that as a starting point to listen to God's call in your life. And remember that I'm not suggesting you have to leave your current profession. As you make the transition to living out your call to greatness, just be open to how God wants to use you. You can trust absolutely that it will be consistent with the gifts he's given you and that it will fulfill you.

If you don't yet feel as if you have a good sense of your desires, needs, and talents, don't get frustrated. Many are in the same boat, including myself not so long ago. I strongly suggest that you take the subject to prayer. I also recommend seeking counsel from a mentor, family members, and friends, those you can trust to help you discern the gifts you have. Last, pay attention to what's going on around you, how God may be speaking to you through the people and events in your life. God will show you what he wants if you persevere in asking him.

To do God's will, there are three things you have to believe.

1. God loves you more than you love yourself.
2. God knows what's best for you.
3. God wants your happiness more than you do.

It's my hope that by reading this book you are at least beginning to believe all of the above. But words on a page won't do it. You need to experience conversion in a deeply personal way and to understand and internalize God's unconditional love and forgiveness. You need to allow God to heal you and form you. If you're not there yet, don't worry, and don't beat yourself up. Try to follow the various preliminary steps outlined in previous chapters, especially chapter 7. Take your time, recognizing that even though these steps are relatively simple, they're not easy. If you persevere and keep on praying, you will get there.

No matter where you are on the journey, keep trying and keep praying. You can trust in God's unconditional love. You can trust that he made you uniquely and for a special purpose. You can trust that he knows your heart, planted the deepest desires you have, and will fulfill them in and for you in his good time — if you let him.

Our Call to Holiness

You may have come to a place of faith prior to picking up this book. Or perhaps as you've been reading it, you decided to begin to journey with the Lord. Possibly, you are still searching. Regardless, separate from profession or vocation, you may be asking yourself, "What is God calling me to do; who is God calling me to be?"

What is a "vocation"? The definition of the word is "a call." But a vocation is more than an ordinary call. A vocation is a call from God. While most people think of it as what they are called to do in life, it is important to understand that the first and most important call from God is the universal call to holiness.

Your vocation is not the same as your career or profession, though there can be overlap between the two. A career or a profession is something you have in order to support yourself and to contribute in some way to the good of society. You don't need to believe in God to choose a career. A person can pick, choose, and switch professions, freely depending on preferences, strengths, or circumstances. A profession or a career always has a horizontal dimension.

When we talk about vocation, we introduce a vertical dimension in our life. The driving question is then no longer "What do I prefer?" but "What does God want me to be?" The universal call to holiness is a call to know, love, and serve the Lord. It is a movement that draws us into a deeper union with God. We feel a growing desire to love our neighbor. We come to understand that there is a reason for our existence and meaning to our lives. The universal call to holiness is an ongoing conversion experience. It keeps opening our eyes to new awareness of God's loving presence. It keeps inviting us to turn toward God by aligning our will with his.

For Catholics, our call to holiness is a call to live a specific way of life that requires us to give of ourselves in some way. This could be as a single consecrated person, as a married person, as a consecrated religious, as an ordained minister. God calls each of us to walk one of these specific paths, and choosing the one he has planned for us requires courage, discernment, and trust.

The last thing Jesus said before he ascended into heaven was: "Go therefore and make disciples of all nations, baptizing them in the name of the Father and of the Son and of the Holy Spirit, teaching them to observe all that I have commanded you; and behold, I am with you always, to the close of the age" (Mt 28:19–20). Known as the Great Commission, this was not merely a suggestion. It was Jesus' directive to us to share his love with the world, to make disciples. He calls us to minister to those in our sphere of influence, those who are part of our lives, whether family, friends, associates, or acquaintances.

God wants your availability more than your ability. Just look at the people with whom Jesus surrounded himself. They were not pillars of the community or leaders in the Jewish faith. They were not trained or educated. They were fishermen and laborers, and women who were moved by his message, many of whom had been afflicted with diseases, spiritual possession, and lives of sin before they encountered the Lord.

Jesus wasn't looking for their ability. Instead, he was seeking to surround himself with people who would believe in him, who would invest in a relationship with him, and who would have the courage to do his work.

God invites you into this relationship with him. He loves you and wants you to be fulfilled. He wants to carry you beyond the things that have overwhelmed you until now, the fear of not being good enough, the failure to love yourself, the many fears that have held you back. He would like to eliminate your false gods and offer you himself to fill that God-sized hole in the center of your chest. He wants to heal your wounds and relieve your resentments. God wants you to be happy, so that you can live for the specific purpose he had in mind when he created you. Most of all, God wants to be in a personal, intimate relationship with you.

God made you for greatness. He wants to see you thrive, to see you soar, to see you be your very best, to live fulfilled, to experience real joy, and to have peace.

It's never too late to be the person you want to be, the person God calls you to be.

Answer his call. Accept his invitation. Your life will never be the same.

REFLECTION

- What is that one thing that always makes you feel alive when you do it? Where and when have you felt most fully yourself?
- If you're already on a vocational path, how can you live your calling more generously today? Where do you think God might be inviting you to live more fully?

SUGGESTED ACTIONS

- Give prayer time to your unique genius (talents, desires, needs). Ask God, "What is your plan for my life?"

- Make a list of those in your life you can be showing more love to. What are some of the things you can be doing?
- Pray about how you can participate in the Great Commission.
- Now, understanding that you were made for greatness, live your life that way. Make the decision to stop being overwhelmed, but fulfilled, living a life of joy and peace.

NOTES

_____

_____

_____

_____

_____

_____

_____

_____

_____

_____

_____

_____

CONCLUSION

God helps us make a ministry out of our messes. The things that have caused us the most despair, the moments when we were at our worst — these are the parts of our lives that shape us the most for future endeavors.

At Franciscan University, I get to work with the best and most talented Catholic authors and speakers in North America. One of my very favorites, because of the beautiful and authentic person she is, is Sister Miriam James Heidland, a sister of the Society of Our Lady of the Most Holy Trinity (SOLT). (I highly recommend her book, *Loved as I Am*.) She gave the keynote for Steubenville's 2014 Power and Purpose Conference, and her powerful presentation strikes me as the best way to wrap up this book.

Sister Miriam tells a story from *The Voyage of the Dawn Treader* (one of the books in the Chronicles of Narnia by C. S. Lewis). She recounts the tale of Eustace, a mean little boy whose greed and selfishness make everyone around him miserable. At one point during the story, Eustace runs away from his companions because he doesn't want to help with chores. He falls asleep in a dragon's lair and awakens as a dragon. All of the darkness within him is now on the outside for all to see, and much destruction ensues because of his awful transformation. His terrified cousins try to heal him, but to no avail. At his wits' end and losing hope, Eustace encounters the lion Aslan, the Christ figure of the Narnia series. Aslan brings Eustace to a cool, clear pool of water and urges him to undress and get in.

Confused at first because, as a dragon, he is not wearing any clothes, Eustace quickly realizes the ugliness of his scales and begins to scratch at himself. He scratches a layer of the ugliness away and approaches the pool to enter, but upon seeing his reflection, he realizes he is still a dragon. Eustace tries two more times to remove the scales, but after each attempt he sees it is fruitless. We often do the same, scratching at what we find ugly in ourselves, but unable to make it go away.

Failing in his attempts, Eustace finally realizes he cannot fix himself. Upon seeing this, Aslan comments, "You will have to let me undress you." With his paw, the mighty lion pierces the hard shell of the dragon and begins to tear away at the layers of his skin. The pain is initially so deep that Eustace thinks Aslan has pierced his very heart. After some time, the tearing ceases and Eustace looks at the dreadful, thick skin lying in a huge pile beside him. Before he can say anything, Aslan throws him into the pool. Eustace begins to swim, noticing he is free of pain and discomfort. As he looks down at himself, he realizes he is a boy again, no longer a dragon. Eustace is never the same after that encounter with Aslan. He still struggles now and then with some of his old tendencies, but Eustace is profoundly different because of his encounter with Love.

This is the transformation we're invited to undergo. God wants to bring each of us to the place where we can say, like Saint Paul, "I have been crucified with Christ; it is no longer I who live, but Christ who lives in me; and the life I now live in the flesh I live by faith in the Son of God, who loved me and gave himself for me" (Gal 2:20).

The difference between the dragon and the boy is the same difference we encounter between our old selves and our new selves when we really let God transform us. We can leave the sick, fearful, self-centered, seeking old self behind, living in a place of gratitude for everything that happened to us because it brought us to this point. Like Eustace, when we finally let God in to work on us, to transform us, it changes everything.

We are works in progress. None of us can ever say in this

life that we've "made it" — because heaven is the goal, and we can't get there in this life. All we can do is start on the road and renew the journey each day, committing ourselves to God's loving purpose.

God loves us unconditionally. He is in control. He knows us better than we could ever know ourselves, and he loves us infinitely. He invites each of us to play a critical role in his grand plan. Like many before me, God has allowed me to go through experiences, even tragedies, so he could shape me into the person he wants me to be. Each of us is a pencil in the hand of the Lord.

I can't wait to see the story he has yet to write for each one of us.

The unimaginable is achievable when we let go and let God run our lives. Regardless of the obstacles, we can live in peace, joy, and fulfillment, heaven here on earth.

May God bless you on your journey.

PRAYERS

The Serenity Prayer
God grant me the serenity
To accept the things I cannot change;
Courage to change the things I can;
And wisdom to know the difference.

Living one day at a time;
Enjoying one moment at a time;
Accepting hardships as the pathway to peace;
Taking, as He did, this sinful world as it is,
Not as I would have it;
Trusting that He will make all things right
If I surrender to His Will;
So that I may be reasonably happy in this life
And supremely happy with Him forever in the next.
Amen.

— Prayer attributed to Reinhold Neibuhr, 1892–1971

Thank You, God the Father; Thank, You Jesus!
Dear Jesus Christ, Son of the Father, thank you for dying that torturous death on the cross for each one of us, including me. Thank you for rising from the dead so that I can live in your glory.

God the Father, thank you for loving me enough to give me your only-begotten Son.

Lord Jesus, thank you for my journey, every step along the way, the good, the great, the wonderful, the bad, the terrible, the ugly. I am where I am because it is where you want me to be. I am who I am because it is who you are making me to be. I trust in you to make me and shape me for your glory.

Thank you for loving me, blessing me, showing me your will, showering me with your grace, and granting me your peace, which can only come from being in a place of surrender, gratitude, humility, and love.

Lord Jesus, help me to feel your unconditional love and unconditional forgiveness, fully living and internalizing these gifts, so that with Holy Spirit boldness, using my God-given gifts, not caring what anyone on this earth thinks of me, I can be all that you want me to be, in serving you.

Dear Lord, help me always to see Christ in all and be Christ to all, living your will, helping others become the best versions of themselves, which is true love … Christ's love.

Please give me the strength and courage to evangelize my faith, living the Gospel, sharing the Gospel, using words when necessary and always.

When done for the glory of God, the unimaginable is achievable.

I ask this blessing for my family and friends (include names, if desired), for myself, and for all those on your journey … grant us peace. For all those seeking, help them find. For all those lost, help them see.

I ask this in the name of the Father, Son, and Holy Spirit. Amen.

— Composed by Mark Joseph, 2009

Appendix 2

SUGGESTED READING

Jason Evert, *Saint John Paul the Great: His Five Loves*. San Francisco: Ignatius Press, 2014.

Sr. Miriam James Heidland, SOLT, *Loved as I Am: An Invitation to Conversion, Healing, and Freedom through Jesus*. Notre Dame, Ind.: Ave Maria Press, 2014.

Matthew Kelly, *The Rhythm of Life: Living Every Day with Passion and Purpose, third edition*. North Palm Beach, Fla., Beacon Publishing, 2015.

Fr. Jacques Philippe, *Searching for and Maintaining Peace: A Small Treatise on Peace of Heart*. Staten Island, N.Y.: Alba House, 2002.

Fr. Michael Scanlan, TOR, *Let the Fire Fall*, third edition. Steubenville, Ohio: Franciscan University of Steubenville, 2016.

Deacon Keith Strohm, *Jesus: The Story You Thought You Knew*. Huntington, Ind.: Our Sunday Visitor, 2017.

Rev. Rick Warren, *The Purpose Driven Life*. Grand Rapids, Mich.: Zondervan, 2002.

ACKNOWLEDGMENTS

I have so many friends who have helped me on this journey, many of whom reviewed early drafts of the book, including Brian Conboy, Tony Cotrupi, Gabe Difurio, Pete Diulus, Leon Dwinga, Jay Fairbrother, Jim Hanna, Len Petrancosta, Dan Raeder, Fr. Shawn Roberson, TOR, Larry Sipos, and others who I've inevitably, unintentionally forgotten. To all, a sincere thank you!!!

Thank you, Randy Raus and John Zimmer, who not only reviewed the book, but have been brothers in Christ and always there for me. The same is true for Fr. Paul Zywan and Fr. Nathan Malavolti, TOR.

Thank you to all who endorsed this book, in addition to those I have the privilege of working with at Franciscan University of Steubenville, including our Steubenville speakers and worship leaders, all of whom have positively impacted my journey.

This project would have never gotten off the ground without the generosity and guidance of Paul George, Mark Hart, Chris Padgett, and Lynn Wehner. All four spent hours coaching me and working with me. I am forever indebted to them for their friendship and advice.

Dr. Elaine Malec, my therapist, will always hold a special place in my heart. She not only patiently worked with me to understand and internalize God's unconditional love, but helped me to identify his plan for my life. I could not have asked for a better "guide" for the journey, someone who strongly challenged me where appropriate and compassionately worked with me to finally love myself in a healthy, Christ-like way.

I'd like to thank OSV for publishing this book and Mary Beth Baker, my editor, for her guidance and support. Not just unique to writing, she taught me that "less is more" and "the message has to stand on its own." The best compliment I can offer is that I'd love to work with Mary Beth again.

Cyndi and I, as husband and wife, are best friends and soul mates on this journey of life. I love her immensely and am forever grateful for her support. Likewise, I cherish our three kids, ever so appreciative of their love and encouragement. Thank you to my parents and brothers (Dan, Chris, and Tom), the only ones who have witnessed my journey from the beginning. Thank you for always loving me.

Finally, I'd like to thank Our Lord for his unconditional love and forgiveness, in addition to the plan he so clearly has for my life. I am blessed abundantly.